# UNACCOUNTABLE CONGRESS

## It Doesn't Add Up

Joseph J. DioGuardi, CPA

Member of Congress

1985-88

2010 Update

With new Foreword by the author

Library of Congress Cataloging-In-Publication Data

DioGuardi, Joseph J., 1940—
Unaccountable Congress : it doesn't add up / Joseph J. DioGuardi.
p.     cm.
Includes bibliographical references and index.
ISBN 978-0-89526-521-0
1. Waste in government spending—United States.     2. Finance,
Public—United States—Accounting.   3. United States. Congress
I. Title
HJ7537.D55     1992
336.73 —dc20                            91-43617
CIP

Originally published in the United States by
Regnery Gateway
1130 17th Street, NW
Washington, DC 20036




2010 printing
Manufactured in the United States of America

# FOREWORD

When *Unaccountable Congress: It Doesn't Add Up* was first published in 1992, the Chief Financial Officers Act that I authored as a New York Congressman had been signed by President George H.W. Bush just two years earlier. It seemed like the government's standards for financial reporting might be improving, and that we were headed for real reform. The bill had been watered down some, but it still created a chief financial officer for each of the federal departments and agencies, and gave the Office of Management and Budget more control. The future had the potential to be brighter and the taxpayers more informed about where our money was going.

Now, at the 20th anniversary of the Chief Financial Officers Act, our government continues to operate behind closed doors regarding its budgeting process, the national debt is skyrocketing out of control into the trillions, and we recently witnessed a near collapse of the entire U.S. economy—thanks to the same old shell games in Congress. We still haven't learned the lessons of the past regarding accountability in federal budgeting, and as a result we continue to stare into the heart of a "gathering storm" (to use the prophetic words of Winston Churchill). But most important, we aren't addressing the root cause of our massive debt: bloated government, which, if the current Congress has its way, will only expand more. In the absence of sound accounting and sound budgeting, we lack information for decision-making and invite gimmickry and half-measures, rather than leadership.

We must act now to keep our country solvent. The situation is urgent. The President, his cabinet, the members of the House and Senate can pretend in front of TV cameras that we have the luxury of time and that we need only increase our debt ceiling by another trillion or two, and the country will be fine—but they know that our economy is literally living on borrowed time and borrowed money. The big spenders in Congress believe that bigger government is the answer, and they keep pushing up the ceiling on the national debt.

Now the good news: the American people are smart. They know that smaller government is the answer, and they are willing to get off the couch and get involved to create the government they want.

## THE SCOTT HEARD 'ROUND THE WORLD

As of this writing, the biggest surprise in the Obama-era political arena has been the January 2010 election in Massachusetts of Scott Brown to the Senate seat previously occupied by the late Edward Kennedy for more than 45 years. The moderate Republican ran a positive campaign based not only on defeating the healthcare bill, but also on account-ability and reform. The voters of Massachusetts who sent Brown to the Senate signaled the seismic shift in the U.S. political atmosphere at that moment; more citizens, particularly independent-minded people in all political parties, are finding constructive ways to express their anger at the unaccountable Congress and the Obama administration's agenda of more intrusive government.

The surge in citizen activism is personified by the Tea Party move-ment, which started primarily as a reaction to healthcare reform legisla-tion. When the Obama administration and Congressional representatives dismissed the first Tea Party march in April 2009, the activists' resolve only strengthened and their numbers grew. The mission expanded from exercising First Amendment rights to making Congress more respon-sive to their electorate. The Tea Party movement attracted and energized the fiscal conservatives in Massachusetts to secure a shock victory for Brown in the U.S. Senate race.

While Brown's victory is certainly a significant example of the kind of grassroots activism needed to push the government to act in the na-tion's best interests, many of these citizen activists may not be com-pletely informed as to why the national debt is ballooning out of control, or the specific actions that need to be taken to ensure government ac-countability with their tax dollars.

The best way to understand how our national debt affects you as a taxpayer is to think about it in simple terms. If you or your family need to spend more in a month than your actual income, you might borrow money that you will have to repay at a certain interest rate. If you keep doing this, or do not make full and timely payments, your interest costs will rise and eventually exceed anything else in your budget. This is what is happening to the United States; President Obama admitted as much to Steve Scully on C-SPAN in May 2009 when he said, "We are out of money now."

## IN WASHINGTON, NOTHING IS CERTAIN BUT DEBT & TAXES

Our reported national debt has grown from around $800 billion in 1980—which took two centuries to accumulate—to just over $12 trillion as of September 30, 2009, less than 30 years later. The Obama administration freely admits that it will rise to $20 trillion by 2020—unless we act now. It's been a mind-boggling increase, fueled by the ever-burgeoning size of the U.S. government and the even more staggering amount owed for entitlement programs such as Social Security and Medicare. Do we really need 16 intelligence agencies, especially when their combined efforts couldn't keep the Christmas Day terrorist off the plane to Detroit? To repeat what I said originally in Chapter 4 of this book, the spiraling deficit will render the United States economy unsustainable and in need of a bailout itself.

Why? Because the interest alone on a $20 trillion debt will be more than $1 trillion per year at current interest rates, and these rates will almost certainly rise. Then we'll have the problem of unrecorded and unfunded liabilities such as Social Security and Medicare, currently estimated at $45 trillion. These programs tend to disappear from the discussion because they are effectively kept off the government's books and annual financial reports. Worse yet, "baby boomers" in the process of retiring are beginning to receive their benefits now. As of this writing, Social Security will—for the first time, and *six years earlier than expected*—pay out more in Social Security benefits than it receives in payments. And since we still don't have outside auditors coming in to oversee government budgeting, spending, and reporting, it's hard to tell whether future retirees will receive all of the money promised them.

Every year since 1969, Congress has spent more than the revenue it has brought in and the number of government agencies and programs has expanded, creating a mountain of debt on which the Treasury

Department must pay interest. The budget "surpluses" claimed by the Clinton administration weren't surpluses at all—Clinton used the "unified budget approach" started originally by President Lyndon Johnson for the purpose of concealing the real cost of the Vietnam War. Johnson offset the surpluses in the Social Security Trust Fund against the deficit from U.S. government operations in order to show a better result. The same shell game is at work today, but now the Medicare Trust Fund surpluses are also being used to reduce the size of the budget deficit.

In the fiscal year 2009, the Treasury spent $383 billion of your tax dollars on interest to holders such as China and Japan. And you wonder why social services or crucial infrastructures such as our roads are in dire need of help? Compare that $383 billion in interest to the paltry $73 billion for the entire Department of Transportation last year; we're already paying a disproportionate amount for interest and receive no service for the expense.

In order for businesses to hire new workers, they need tax breaks and consumer spending—not more tax increases, which are inevitable as interest on the debt grows to become the biggest item in the federal budget. These tax increases will also cause the inflation of consumer goods as corporations pass cost increases on to the consumer. This is the last thing a country struggling with high unemployment needs. To sum things up, the size of the national debt affects the interest rates for borrowing and investing, the federal income tax paid, the price each of us pays for groceries and other goods, as well as the unemployment rate. For all intents and purposes, the national debt is the 800-pound gorilla in the room.

U.S. Senator Sam Brownback from Kansas recently pointed out an important new study presented at the American Economic Association ("Growth in a Time of Debt") that shows how high national debt bodes poorly for any country's economic growth. He concluded that annual growth in U.S. gross domestic product (GDP) has averaged considerably less than 4% over the past 10 years, and that "carrying a high national debt could mean the difference between a growing economy and a contracting economy." Our national debt is expected to exceed 90 percent of GDP this year, and 100 percent within the next decade—that's not even considering the huge liabilities for Social Security and Medicare.

# ASK AN ACCOUNTANT

As the first practicing Certified Public Accountant (CPA) elected to Congress, I have long tried to call attention to our inadequate federal budgeting, accounting, and reporting practices. While in Congress during the late 1980s, I served on both the House Government Operations and Banking Committees, where I learned firsthand that government entities use gimmicky shell games similar to those special purpose entities employed by Enron—a disgraced company that used blatant subterfuges to hide its growing losses and debt. In Washington, these special purpose entities are called Government Sponsored Enterprises (GSEs), and include companies such as the Resolution Trust Corporation, which was used to implement the massive off-budget bailout during the Savings and Loan scandal of the late 1980s. More recently, two other GSEs—Fannie Mae and Freddie Mac—were used to fuel the subprime mortgage and toxic securities scandals, leading to massive amounts of government bailout money in the form of federal guarantees of their bonds.

In a *Washington Times* op-ed piece published on August 24, 2009, I wrote that "the financial management failures of U.S. corporations cannot come close to rivaling the budget and bookkeeping shambles of the U.S. government." I went on to explain that the hole in our nation's finances is really $56 trillion once the unrecorded liabilities of about $45 trillion from Medicare and Social Security are factored into the equation. This number is a far cry from the $12 trillion national debt publicized by the government's balance sheets, which leave off financial manipulations on a scale that dwarfs those of the Enron scandal.

America has a national debt of gargantuan proportions because of the unaccountability of Congress, unbridled deregulation during the Bush-Cheney administration, and accelerated spending of both political parties. The debt situation is even worse when you consider the operating deficits of GSEs whose debt is backed by the full faith and credit of the U.S. Treasury.

## IT'S DEREGULATION TIME, SO WHO'S MINDING THE STORE?

Just what has happened in the fiscal realm since I left Congress in 1989? A chronology of important events following this foreword illustrates my point: Congress has continued to spend as if there is no tomorrow, and our

Congressional representatives use their plastic voting cards as a collective "credit card" to provide the juice—like illegal steroid use in professional sports—that keeps their jobs in Washington, while taxpayers remain in the dark about what is really going on.

In 1999, we saw the repeal of the Glass-Steagall Act, created in the wake of the Great Depression to separate investment and commercial banks. Once repealed, there was effective deregulation of the banking, insurance, and securities industries, which allowed financial institutions to become "too big to fail."

Writers and opinion-makers have said that the highest impact financial event during the crisis of the past few years was the subprime mortgage crisis, which began in 2007. Stock markets plunged and credit froze in September 2008. As a remedy, U.S. Treasury Secretary Henry Paulson proposed a sweeping $700 billion dollar bailout of our financial institutions: The Troubled Asset Relief Program (TARP).

Struggling Americans who had to give up their homes didn't enjoy learning that huge banks were being bailed out, but Federal Reserve Chairman Ben Bernanke claimed at the time that we might have been only three days away from our entire economy collapsing. Of course, this would have had disastrous ripple effects around the world. Something had to be done, and so Congress, along with the American people, held its collective nose and approved the massive bailouts *without any due diligence*.

There's a common thread here that I began to unwind in the original printing of this book and it's still unraveling today. Former government interventions (the S&L bailout of 1987, the Farm Aid crises in the early 1980s, and the New York City bailout in 1975) used the "full faith and credit" of the federal government to float bonds backed by the U.S. Treasury. We have continued this tradition by bailing out "too big to fail" companies without passing legislation to prevent similar catastrophes in the future. Worse still, we have not properly accounted for the cost of these bailouts, leaving the next generation to figure out how to pay for our profligacy.

## HOW MUCH ARE BAILOUTS REALLY COSTING US?

Regarding the subprime mess, the Federal Reserve failed to use its supervisory and regulatory authority over banks, mortgage underwriters, and other lenders. Fannie Mae and Freddie Mac, the nation's two largest mortgage finance lenders, had to be essentially nationalized—placed under the conservatorship of the Federal Housing Finance Agency with money authorized by the Housing and Economic Recovery Act of 2008. Accountants and Congressional oversight forces were not doing their jobs. They allowed huge loans to be written without the proper reserves and adequate accounting, which led to the biggest banking crisis debacle since the Great Depression.

The price tag for the widespread bailouts has been an ongoing source of consternation, if not real outrage, from the public. One problem seldom discussed in the press is that no one knows the real size of the bailout. Estimates vary depending on who is reporting. (*The New York Times* reported in September 2009 that the government has "rolled out more than a dozen programs and made commitments of about $12.5 trillion to protect the economy from crisis.")

Economist and journalist Nomi Prins found that, after crunching the hidden numbers, the size of the bailout was $14.4 trillion and counting. In her most recent book, *It Takes a Pillage: Behind the Bailouts, Bonuses, and Backroom Deals from Washington to Wall Street*, Prins presents charts that show $7.2 trillion flowing through the Treasury Department (mostly to Money Market Mutual and Public-Private Investment Funds) and $7.2 trillion through the Federal Reserve (mostly for Commercial Paper Funding Facility, mortgage-backed securities purchase, and Term Asset-Backed Securities Loan Facility).

What's a few trillion here or there? Well, it's a lot for the taxpayer, and it's something that shouldn't be difficult for citizens to trace and account for. As columnist George Will said, "The essence of this crisis is lack of knowledge, including the inability to know who owes what to whom, and where risk resides." Americans demand the most from their favorite contestants on hit shows like *American Idol*; shouldn't we demand the most from politicians saddling our children's future with enormous debt?

The risk issue George Will mentioned is just as critical to U.S. financial sustainability as the need for accurate reports of the monies loaned, monies printed, assets purchased, and liabilities backed by the U.S. government. The truth is that the bailouts are transfers of wealth from the government (all citizens) to a particular industry (namely, the banking industry) and its backers. The long-term effects of transfers of wealth need to be understood before they occur.

Columnist Gretchen Morgenson stated (*New York Times*,

April 26, 2010), "A major factor missing from Treasury's math is the vast transfer of wealth to banks from investors resulting from the Fed's near-zero interest-rate policy." The Fed's stimulus policy allows banks to borrow at ridiculously low interest rates (.25 percent) in order to encourage the banks to lend money to businesses and consumers at affordable rates. But the banks aren't doing it! Instead, they're lending the money BACK to the U.S. government by purchasing Treasury bills at 3 percent and making money on the point spread. They're charging consumers an average of 14 percent interest on credit cards, and making even more money on this point spread.

The economic impact is, according to Andrew Haldane, Executive Director of Financial Stability at the Bank of England, a long-term, significant reduction in the U.S. GDP. In March 2010 at the Institute of Regulation & Risk, Haldane dubbed these results "banking pollution." Congress must take into account the long-term economic impact and take steps to reduce this pollution, but will it?

Let's take a look at what Congress and the Obama Administration are doing to respond to public anger and concern. Congress established a Financial Crisis Inquiry Commission chaired by Phil Angelides, a former state treasurer of California, where unemployment and foreclosure rates are among the highest in the nation. The commission has been grilling the heads of the financial companies who benefited from the bailouts, even though many have repaid (with interest) the funds they received. President Obama appears to be catering to public anger by conjuring up a "revenge tax" on banks. Neither one of these approaches will yield a constructive solution to our current situation. The President has also proposed establishing a new agency to protect consumers — spending even *more* taxpayer money and creating more debt.

We have built an economic "house of cards" on negative personal savings rates, excessive consumption, spending beyond our means — both individually and as a nation — and now that house is falling in every direction. It's not a matter of opinion — even the International Monetary Fund has warned about the threat to the global financial system because of the reliance on debt. The U.S. has hard work to do to clean up the mess, but if we start now, we can succeed.

# CONGRESS: BREEDING GROUND OF THE DOUBLE STANDARD

Are you surprised that Congress won't live by the same budgeting, accounting, and reporting standards that it requires of everyone else? I discovered this during my years in Congress and wrote about it in the original book.

As far back as 1956, the second Hoover Commission foresaw the problem, and actually did something about it that could have worked. It pushed Congress to amend the 1950 Budget and Accounting Procedures Act to require all government agencies to maintain their accounts on the "accrual basis" to record commitments to spend in the future, as well as current spending. The Securities and Exchange Commission imposes this method, known as "generally accepted accounting principles" (GAAP), on publicly traded companies. Congress never implemented this important amendment, and as a result we have had a double standard between private sector and government budgeting, accounting, and reporting for more than 50 years.

The accounting system we have failed to rectify has, in effect, created what I call a "subprime national debt," and a good deal of the money you pay in taxes goes toward paying interest on that debt. When Republicans took over the House of Representatives in 1994, they voted *on the first day* to have Price Waterhouse conduct an audit of House finances. In its first audit report, Price Waterhouse found that the House "lacks the organization and structure to periodically prepare financial statements that...are accurate and reliable" and that financial management information was "simplistic and ill-suited" for an organization with a billion dollar budget, and that it *could not be audited*.

I called it a "smoking gun" when the late Robert Novak interviewed me for his 1995 documentary film, *America the Bankrupt*. Nothing has changed since then. This double standard and the problems it creates for the American people were so disturbing that I founded Truth In Government, a non-profit organization dedicated to bringing appropriate accounting standards in Congress. Over the past two decades I have traveled the country, revealing what Congress really does and really spends, and demanding that business and civic groups pay attention to the need for change.

My message has not changed: It is crucial for us to restore integrity to the budgeting process and provide financial accountability to the taxpayers. The challenges that we face are so great, that only a shared commitment will make it happen. These are perilous times that require unified effort and leadership, but today's politicians cannot muster the political will to confront the nation's financial problems.

## SEND CONGRESS TO ACCOUNTING REFORM SCHOOL

Congressional budgeting, accounting, and reporting practices must be changed. I've been saying this since I learned what Congress was actually doing when I served there. In 1993 I chaired a Task Force on Emerging Issues, sponsored by the Association of Government Accountants. Here's my statement in the report:

> At a time when Congress must make important decisions on future budget priorities and commitments, the information necessary to make those decisions is woefully defective. Weak government-wide budgeting and accounting systems produce insufficient reliable information about how the government spends its funds and how decisions made today will affect tomorrow's taxpayers. Further, the Congressional budgeting process commonly relies upon imaginary revenues, ignores unfunded obligations, and makes use of numerous other practices lacking economic and accounting reality. The Federal government badly needs major budgeting reforms.

The task force recommended the six reforms listed below, none of which have been adopted *more than 17 years later*. If we had adopted even some of these reforms, we could have prevented the mess in which we find ourselves today:

- Employ generally accepted accounting principles (GAAP), beginning with the budget process, before money is committed or spent.
- Adopt separate budgets for general funds, trust funds, and GSEs. (Overall, such tripartite reporting would give Congress and the public a far more accurate picture of the federal government's spending activities.)
- Adopt effective capital budgeting, which is a financial process used to plan, control, record, and report long-term capital expenditures.
- Adopt biennial budget cycles corresponding to a Congressional term of office. (This would require Congress to authorize spending only once in two years and allow more time for needed oversight.)
- Maintain the Budget Enforcement Act of 1990. (If discretionary

spending in any of three categories—defense, international, domestic—exceeds the Act's target as of the beginning of a fiscal year, an automatic sequester is applied to that category to stop spending from other federal sources to cover it.)

- Publicize the true financial condition of the federal government and an accurate report of the results of *all* the operations of the federal government each year.

In order to stop the games Congress plays to minimize the real financial impact of its legislation, we need to have the President's budgetary proposals and Congressional bills evaluated for their financial impact by the Government Accountability Office, an independent agency headed by the non-political Comptroller General of the United States. We absolutely need a *concise*, GAAP-consistent report on the operation and financial condition of the U.S. government, including all its revenues, expenditures, assets, and liabilities, that would be made readily available to the public and news media shortly after each September 30, the end of the federal government's fiscal year.

## WISDOM OF THE FOUNDERS: LIMIT GOVERNMENT

During the first year of the Obama Administration, we watched a messy political drama unfold over healthcare reform. Congressional representatives didn't listen (and still aren't listening) to their constituents who want smaller government and less intrusion. They argued about how to fund this largely unpopular initiative more than whether we could or should pay for it. They ignored major vehicles for lowering health care costs: tort reform and reducing defensive medicine practices. The members of Congress who voted for the recently enacted healthcare law knew that its purported savings were not likely to be realized. Less than one month after the President signed the healthcare bill into law, the government's own Centers for Medicare and Medicaid Services announced that the costs of the bill will exceed Congress' projections by $311 billion over the first nine years. No matter what the people want, Congress continues to raise taxes and mislead the American people they are supposed to represent.

In 2010, many Americans are hurting—especially the middle class and the poor. Housing has not fully recovered, our commercial real estate market is starting to feel the pain in big cities, and we have an unemployment level at 10 percent and growing—the highest since 1982, according to recent Bureau of Labor Statistics data. (The unemployment number is actually higher, considering how many people are now working part-time or have stopped searching out of frustration or hopelessness.) Ironically, we still haven't seen fit to look at our financial problems with transparency and accountability, utilizing the finest financial management practices and principles of accounting. We have not addressed redundancies in government programs—one of the first strategies businesses use when they reduce costs.

One of the greatest lessons I learned while in Congress was that our founding fathers, the framers of the U.S. Constitution, got it right. They deliberately limited the power of the federal government in order to preserve freedom and limit the burden of paying taxes, which had been a major source of discontent before The Revolution. Limiting federal government power means limiting its size—an idea that has been forgotten or systematically rejected in the past 100 years. The healthcare reform issue jolted many Americans out of the big government mindset, and now we need to chart a new course for prosperity.

The elections of fiscal conservatives in the 2009 New Jersey and Virginia gubernatorial races and in the 2010 Senate race in Massachusetts serve as a bellwether for our future. Other positive signs indicate that we are beginning to reject huge deficit spending and limit the size of government. Emerging leaders such as Rep. Paul Ryan of Wisconsin have proposed solutions for balancing the budget and reducing Medicare costs. Rep. Frank Wolf and Rep. Jim Cooper have jointly proposed forming a bipartisan panel to address the budget crisis and "put all options on the table." Truth In Government will contribute to this new, positive direction by creating a plan for job growth and fiscal sustainability.

For the past 20 years, I've been beating the drum for greatly needed reform, and now America is waking up. We the people can be a force for America's sustainable future, if we demand that Congress make the changes Truth In Government has identified, balance the budget, and generate real jobs.

Joe DioGuardi
Ossining, New York
May 2010

## POSTSCRIPT

As we go to press, Europe is experiencing its own financial crisis. Greece's history of deficit spending on a bloated civil service and disproportionately large pensions has left it teetering on the edge of bankruptcy, and in need of an emergency bailout of $145 billion from the European Union and the International Monetary Fund. In order to receive the funds, Greece had to agree to an austerity program of cuts that resulted in protests and violence. Citizens of the European Union countries that financed the bailout are angry that they are assuming the burden for Greece's profligacy.

Portugal and Spain are not far behind. Even the U.K.'s AAA rating is in jeopardy. This scenario is our future, if we do not act now to reduce deficit spending and the national debt and we do not demand that Congress act truthfully and responsibly to protect our future.

## TRUTH IN GOVERNMENT'S 5-POINT PLAN
(from www.TruthInGovernment.org)

1. **Develop a fair and accurate budgeting, accounting, and reporting process based on accrual accounting.** Convert the current cash basis accounting system used in the annual Congressional budgeting process to the system of "generally accepted accounting principles" (GAAP) required of publicly traded corporations by the Securities and Exchange Commission.

2. **Publish clear and accurate information on the finances of the federal government annually.** Use GAAP to disclose all spending and commitments to spend, ensuring that our national debt to foreign sources is clearly delineated.

3. **Make the Chief Financial Officer (CFO) function a Cabinet-level position** and remove financial management and reporting functions from the Treasury Department, transferring them to the nation's CFO, who should immediately engage independent auditors.

4. **Create a new, independent body like the Federal Reserve System** to promulgate sound budgeting and accounting that will prevent political manipulation and conflicts of interest, *removing once and for all* the perennial confusion about the real size of our annual budget deficits and our national debt.

5. **Urge Congress to implement meaningful budgeting, accounting, reporting, and auditing reforms *now*.**

# SELECTED CHRONOLOGY OF EVENTS SINCE 1992: THE "GATHERING STORM" OF THE U.S. FINANCIAL CRISIS

**1992:** Federal Housing Enterprises Financial Safety and Soundness Act creates Office of Federal Housing Enterprise Oversight within the U.S. Dept. of Housing and Urban Development (HUD). Mandates that HUD set goals for Fannie Mae and Freddie Mac regarding low-income housing.

**1994:** Riegle-Neal Interstate Banking and Branching Efficiency Act repeals the Bank Holding Company Act of 1956 that regulated bank holding companies; allows interstate mergers between "adequately capitalized and managed banks, subject to concentration limits, state laws and Community Reinvestment Act (CRA) evaluations."

**1995:** CRA allows mortgage lenders to get credit toward affordable-housing lending obligations for buying subprime securities. This leads to banks lending to higher risk people with bad credit, causing the subprime market to grow.

**1997:** Freddie Mac helps First Union Capital Markets and Bear Stearns & Co. launch the first publicly available securitization of CRA loans.

**1998:** U.S. hedge fund Long-Term Capital Management experiences massive losses due to bond defaults by the Russian government—causing U.S. Treasury Secretary Robert Rubin and the Fed to organize $3.6 billion in bailouts due to the panicked world economy.

**1999:** Gramm-Leach-Bliley Act: "Financial Services Modernization Act" repeals the Glass-Steagall Act and deregulates the banking, insurance, and securities industries. Financial institutions continue to grow even larger.

**2000:** Commodity Futures Modernization Act of 2000 allows trading of credit default swaps with little or no oversight. This is where the buyer in a credit derivative contract gets paid when the underlying investment defaults.

**2000-2001:** Corporate scandals of Enron, WorldCom, Adelphi and Tyco garner widespread media attention and public vilification. Many employees lose their jobs and retirement savings.

**2000-2001:** "Dot com" bubble bursts. The Federal Reserve lowers federal interest rates 11 times, from 6.5 percent to 1.75 percent, creating an easy credit environment fueled by subprime mortgages.

**2001:** September 11—The U.S. is attacked by al-Qaeda; more than 3,000 innocent people are killed. The World Trade Center buildings are reduced to rubble. The Pentagon is severely damaged.

**2002:** Fannie Mae and Freddie Mac start buying subprime mortgages.

**2002:** Investors begin buying more houses, inflating the value of the housing market as demand surges.

**2003:** Bush administration recommends moving government supervision of Fannie Mae and Freddie Mac from Congress to a new agency with Treasury; changes are blocked by Congress.

**2004:** Mortgage-backed securities start being issued more frequently after the SEC lifts leveraging restrictions. Securities, which can now be priced much higher than actual value, push investors to wrongly assume home prices will keep rising for the foreseeable future.

**2006:** Interest rates rise and mortgage loan terms change, triggering the beginning of the widespread foreclosures from homeowners who can no longer afford their mortgages. Most subprime loans increase their interest rates after a few years. The blame game begins.

**2007:** Subprime mortgage fiasco reaches crisis level with 25 mortgage firms declaring bankruptcy. We learn that many banks and global hedge funds were exposed to these asset-backed securities that lacked economic reality and as a result had gone and continue to go bad.

**2008:** January—Global stock markets suffer their biggest drop since Sept. 11, 2001, and the U.S. sees the largest drop in home sales in more than two decades. People in hard-hit cities like Stockton, CA, simply begin abandoning their homes; more and more homes go on the market and newer built homes that sit unoccupied are looted, adversely affecting neighborhoods and prices.

**2008:** March 16—The Federal Reserve and Treasury broker a deal for JPMorgan Chase & Co. to buy Bear Stearns, which was close to collapse—the first brokerage rescue since the Great Depression.

**2008:** July 11—California-based IndyMac Bank, the ninth largest mortgage lender, fails due to loan defaults and a run on deposits.

**2008:** September 7—The nation's financial system begins free fall. Fannie Mae and Freddie Mac are essentially nationalized, placed under the conservatorship of the Federal Housing Finance Agency with funding authorized by the Housing and Economic Recovery Act of 2008.

**2008:** September 15—Lehman Brothers files for bankruptcy.

**2008:** September 16—U.S. government bails out AIG.

**2008:** September 19—Treasury Secretary Henry Paulson proposes the Troubled Assets Relief Program (TARP) to buy troubled assets at discounts from financial institutions that are then made whole.

**2008:** October 3—Congress passes the Emergency Economic Stabilization Act, which authorizes the Treasury Department to spend $700 billion to combat the financial crisis. It begins distributing TARP money through various programs.

**2009:** February 17—Newly elected Democratic President Barack Obama signs $787 billion stimulus package into law.

**2009:** June 1—American iconic car company GM declares bankruptcy, requiring a high "investment" (bailout) from the federal government.

**2009:** June 17—The Treasury Department releases its proposal for reforming financial regulatory system and receives heavy criticism for not doing enough.

**2010:** January—The Treasury Department has given out $247 billion to over 700 banks. As of this writing, $162 billion of that amount has been repaid.

**2010:** January—The Financial Crisis Inquiry Commission convenes to "examine the causes, domestic and global, of the current financial and economic crisis in the United States" and learns little, if anything, from top financial industry executives.

**2010:** January—President Obama calls for a windfall tax that would force banks to pay back bailout funds after seething public resentment at ongoing executive bonuses and record profits.

**2010:** January 19—Continuing a political tsunami that removed the Democratic governors of Virginia and New Jersey from office in the November 2009 elections, the Massachusetts Senate seat that Ted Kennedy held for 46 years is lost to the Republican Party, threatening the Obama administration's healthcare agenda and its profligate deficit spending.

**2010:** January 27—A Congressional Committee questioned Treasury Secretary Tim Geithner about why AIG needed to be bailed out with payments of 100% on its now worthless assets, instead of allowed to go bankrupt. Meanwhile, the Federal Reserve refuses to release documents such as emails that would reveal to U.S. taxpayers about the rationale of the AIG bailout.

**2010:** January 27—President Obama delivers his State of the Union address. The President has now squandered an entire year, and explained the effectiveness of his stimulus bill as "it could have been worse." The unemployment rate went up despite the largest spending increase in U.S. history, and now Congress wants an increase in the debt ceiling substantially more than the entire deficit of $1.4 trillion in the most recent fiscal year (2009).

**2010:** March 23—After contentious debate in both houses of Congress, President Obama signs into law sweeping healthcare legislation, the Patient Protection and Affordable Care Act. The Obama administration praised the bill for its estimated $138 billion deficit reduction over 10 years, even as they added more than $10 trillion to the national debt in the same period (after significant tax increases).

**2010:** April 16—The Securities and Exchange Commission files a lawsuit against Goldman Sachs related to securities backed by subprime mortgages.

**2010:** April 20—The International Monetary Fund holds a news conference to announce that the increased public debt from government interventions (bailouts) threatens the global financial system.

**2010:** April 22—The Department of Health and Human Services' Centers for Medicare and Medicaid Services announces that the costs of the Patient Protection and Affordable Care Act will exceed Congress' projections by $311 billion over the first nine years.

**2010:** November elections—A new beginning for America fueled by an energized electorate *OR* the beginning of the end for the America our founding fathers envisioned?

**2010:** November 16—Twentieth anniversary of the Chief Financial Officer and Federal Financial Management Reform Act (the "CFO Act"), authored and first introduced in the House of Representatives by Joe DioGuardi on March 25, 1986.

# A Congressional voting card is the most expensive credit card in the world.

# Debt Is Making Us Poor

by Joe DioGuardi

**E**very year, the U.S. government runs a deficit, which it adds to the accumulated national debt. The effect is that people don't realize how much the government is actually spending. But what if the government had to tell you just what that shortfall was every year?

As a certified public accountant and former member of Congress, I believe that every citizen has the right to know the real cost of government. So I've converted the annual budget of the United States into a credit card statement.

Note there is a regrettably large previous balance due on your account. This is your share of past spending. When your real credit card company notices that you have reached your limit, it cuts you off. Not so with Congress.

Maybe that would change if we had understandable financial statements mailed to all taxpayers. Then we could talk about moving Election Day to April 15.

*The Washington Post, 1997*

# U.S. Taxpayer
## Congressional Credit Card Statement

| U.S. Government<br>Washington, D.C. | John & Mary Taxpayer<br>Anytown, USA |
|---|---|

### Fiscal Year 2009
#### October 1, 2008 - September 30, 2009

| DESCRIPTION | CHARGES | PAYMENTS |
|---|---|---|
| **PREVIOUS BALANCE DUE** | $554,157* | |
| (Your Share of the National Debt at Beginning of Year) | | |
| **Purchases During Year (Your Share)** | | |
| Medicare & Medicaid | $7,549 | |
| Social Security | 7,275 | |
| National Defense | 6,368 | |
| TARP and Stimulus | 3,162 | |
| Education & Labor | 1,915 | |
| Civil Service, Military Retirement & Disability | 1,296 | |
| Agriculture, Natural Resources | 1,144 | |
| Veterans Affairs | 955 | |
| Transportation | 730 | |
| Housing & Urban Development (HUD) | 610 | |
| Homeland Security | 517 | |
| Other | 864 | |
| **Payments Received During Year (Your Share)** | | |
| Individual Income Taxes | | $9,153 |
| Social Security Taxes & other contributions | | 8,909 |
| Corporate Income Taxes | | 1,382 |
| Miscellaneous Taxes and Fees | | 1,602 |
| **TOTALS** | **$32,385** | **$21,046** |
| **Finance Charge** | | |
| (Your Share of the Interest on the National Debt) | | |
| Paid directly to the public and | | |
| into public trust funds holding government debt | $3,834 | |
| **TOTAL FINANCE CHARGES** | **$3,834** | |
| **New Balance Due** | $569,330* | |
| (Your Share of the National Debt at the End of Year) | | |

| Previous Balance | Purchases | Finance Charges | Payments | Balance Due |
|---|---|---|---|---|
| $554,157* | $32,385 | $3,834 | $21,046 | $569,330* |

\* Includes each taxpayer's share of $45 trillion for unfunded and unrecorded liabilities for Social Security and Medicare.

Note: This statement originally appeared in *Unaccountable Congress: It Doesn't Add Up* © 1992 by Joseph J. DioGuardi.

This revision was prepared in January 2010, based on the federal government's numbers for fiscal year ended September 30, 2009.

**Joseph J. DioGuardi** began his professional career at Arthur Andersen & Co. in 1962. Elected to Congress from Westchester County, New York in 1984, he served two terms on the House Government Operations Committee and one term on the Banking, Finance, and Urban Affairs Committee. He has served on the boards of directors and as chair of the audit committee of several publicly traded and privately held corporations.

**Truth In Government** is a non-profit organization founded in 1989 by Joe DioGuardi. For more information, visit www.truthingovernment.org.

Truth In Government (a division of The Common Sense Educational Fund, Inc.)

P.O. Box 70

Ossining, NY 10562

(914) 923-4702

Connect with Truth In Government:

 www.facebook.com/TruthInGovt

 twitter.com/TruthInGovt

 www.youtube.com/TruthInGovt

 TruthInGovt.wordpress.com

# CONTENTS

# Preface

# JOEY THE WAITER GOES TO WASHINGTON

It was January 1985 and I still wasn't absolutely sure I was a member of Congress. Neither were a lot of voters in the lower half of Westchester County, New York. A majority of them had put the "X" next to my name just two months earlier, but it took a seemingly endless recount to confirm my victory.

I was not only a freshman congressman but also a 43-year-old rookie politician. The only election I had ever won previously was the presidency of our local neighborhood association in New Rochelle. Still, my roots in the area went deep: the son of Italian-Albanian immigrants, I worked as a child in the family's neighborhood market; I waited tables to help pay for college; I knew many people through my profession, and many more through my community activities. As I campaigned against a seemingly unbeatable opponent, I found strength in the hard-working people of my area—some of whom marveled that their "Joey the Waiter" was going to Washington and "straighten those guys out."

When I arrived in the Capitol, about the only thing I knew about serving in Congress was that new members like me were expected to sit down and keep quiet until called upon. Often that wait was long. In fact, there were stories—probably exaggerated—about congressmen who came to Washington, served two decades, and retired, seemingly content, without ever being called upon.

With this knowledge, I attended my first House Republican Conference meeting. Sitting in the cavernous House Caucus Room among some 175 of my colleagues, I listened attentively to the discussion, resolved not to become tagged as "the new guy with the big mouth." Unfortunately, the subject soon swerved into fiscal policy and the federal budget. Several members launched into a debate over how House Republicans might use the budget process to embarrass the "tax-and-spend" Democrats and give an advantage to President Reagan.

As the discussion grew heated, I found it harder to stay quiet. In this room of lawyers I was the sole accountant, in fact the only practicing Certified Public Accountant ever elected to the House or Senate. I had been a partner in Arthur Andersen & Co., one of the "Big Eight" international accounting firms. I had had 22 years experience with income statements, balance sheets, tax returns and audit reports for some of the largest corporations in America. I knew about the accounting gimmicks and financial shenanigans these congressmen were considering. In fact, in my election campaign, I had promised to illuminate the dark fiscal corners of Washington with the light of sound accounting and financial management know-how. Westchester voters seemed to think that was a good idea. Certainly, I thought, my colleagues would as well.

Abandoning my comfortable invisibility, I cleared my throat, stood up and got Conference Chairman Jack Kemp's attention to speak.

"Look," I said, "I may be new around here, but I am a CPA, and I must tell you that the real deficit is much larger than you think, and the smoke and mirrors budgeting you're talking about would get corporate officials sent to jail. How can the people of the United States have confidence in their Congress when it promotes this kind of deceit in something as important as an $800 billion national budget? The other party plays these games all the time, but I think they should be made to pay for it. We Republicans ought to stand for truth in government, truth in budgeting and fiscal responsibility. If we don't stick up for the right thing, what's going to become of this great country?"

Then one very respected senior Republican got up and said, somewhat sarcastically, "Joe, you're in Washington now, and it's time you put away those green eyeshades of yours."

Halted momentarily, I retorted, "With all due respect, sir, I'm not going to trade in my green eyeshades for your blinders."

MY VIEWS DIDN'T prevail that day. They still haven't. But after four years in the Congress I came to feel even more strongly that the very soul of American democracy is in danger. It is in danger because Congress cheats on the numbers. Little numbers. Big numbers. Budget numbers. Lending numbers. Liability numbers. Numbers with enough zeroes to capsize our economy.

Unless we—the people—understand what our government is spending and taxing and guaranteeing, we are in very deep trouble. We are living in a fiscal fantasy that, unlike Cinderella, ends unhappily ever after.

The fallout from this goes far beyond the effects of misleading numbers. This fiscal mismanagement undermines the basic integrity of our form of government, the public's perception of government, and the trust "we the people" place in our elected officials. If every American understood how Congress—and, frequently, the Executive branch as well—relentlessly disguises and hides fiscal reality from the people, that knowledge would escalate citizen contempt to an even higher level. Judging by recent polls, Congress already has a bad reputation, brought on by the sneaky pay raise grabs of 1989 and 1991 and the front-page stories of the sexual and ethical performances of a handful of its members. No wonder the Capitol has been called "a House of Ill Repute."

The activities of a great majority of members of Congress do not elicit outrageous headlines. They've seen what can happen: even a powerful Speaker of the House, Jim Wright, was forced to resign in 1989 for ethical improprieties. Congressmen may not have experienced an ethical conversion, but at least most of them will surely think twice before engaging in really scandalous behavior.

Still, no member of Congress has ever been hounded into disgrace and resignation because his or her sneaky budget gimmick was exposed. And yet the phony accounting principles and budget practices Congress delights in are a far greater threat to our country than anyone's sexual escapades or personal enrichment schemes.

They are a far greater threat because they rot the core of government itself.

To protect themselves from the electorate, most members of Congress have modified the Biblical maxim from "Ye shall know the truth, and the truth shall set you free" to "Ye shall *not* know the truth, for the truth will make you *mad*." Well, it's time Americans knew the truth about a Congress that routinely fudges the numbers. Not through carelessness, but by design. Not to pocket the difference, like a bank embezzler, but to shield citizens from facts which if widely known would force massive change in the financial practices of our national government, and perhaps even eliminate the advantages incumbents seem to have in getting reelected.

This book was written to tell the truth about how your government budgets, spends, and accounts for your money. It won't be the whole truth, because bad budgeting, accounting and reporting practices are so pervasive that no one could expose them all in one volume. Nor is this an encyclopedia of fiscal deceptions. It is only a sampler, the broad strokes of a deception that is threatening your economic well-being, your children's and grandchildren's opportunities, and the very future of our republic.


LET ME EXPLAIN how I got to the point of writing this book. It's a story that really begins in 1929, when a poor lad arrived at New York's Ellis Island from the farming village of Greci, Italy. Many generations before, his family had been driven from the mountains of Albania into Italy by the onslaught of the Ottoman Turks. There in southern Italy (where even today, in villages like Greci, many still speak Albanian as well as Italian) they took a new name, DioGuardi. There they struggled to eke out a living from harsh soil, until my father, his three sisters, and their mother decided that their best hope was the bright shining land across the Atlantic—America.

Young Giuseppe DioGuardi, my father, was 15 years old. He had only the equivalent of five years of school in his poor Albanian-Italian village and knew not a word of English. As the man of the family, he had the responsibility for keeping bread on the table. Soon after arriving in America he found himself walking the streets of Harlem, looking for a job. Today it would be easy for a 15-year-old on city streets to fall quickly into an ugly life of larceny, prostitution or drug dealing. But in 1929, for an immigrant lad with a strong character, determination and faith, there was only one choice: hard, honest work.

The times quickly turned bad. The stock market crashed. The Great Depression began. But Dad was a survivor. He worked. He swept. He carried. He cleaned. And from every menial task this poor immigrant lad performed on the streets of New York, he saved a little bit of his earnings.

When his savings became large enough, Dad opened a tiny vegetable stand in Harlem. It prospered, even in the Depression, because Dad worked hard and because his customers came to trust him. Later he moved up to a grocery store in the Tremont section of the Bronx. He took time off (not much) to fall in love with pretty Grace Paparella, whose Italian immigrant parents and sisters had settled on Manhattan's East Side. They were married, and in 1940 I arrived, the first of their three children.

My early life was pretty well mapped out for me. My job was to do what Dad had done at an early age—work in the store. As soon as I was old enough to handle a broom, I started in the floor sweeping business. When I learned my way around the neighborhood, I got into the delivery business. When I could read, I got into the shelf-stocking business. When I learned to count, I found myself at the cash register.

This working childhood gave me the values that my Mom and Dad believed in: hard work, respect for God and family, the need to put something aside for the future, and the capacity to dream of new challenges and greater achievement. I have never once envied those who grew up in prosperous times and circumstances, instead of hours of hard work on the streets of New York City. And I have never once ceased to respect and admire my Dad and Mom for the wonderful example they set for me in those difficult times.

Achieve! That was their expectation for me, and I did my best. I worked hard in school, with gratifying results. I practiced on my accordion daily. Many times before school at Fordham Prep, in the dim hours before dawn, I would go with Dad to the Bronx Terminal Market near Yankee Stadium to load cartons of groceries and crates of produce. During college, for many long hours, evenings and weekends, I waited tables at the Elmwood Country Club and Abe Levine's Larchmont Lodge in Westchester County, where we moved in 1957. Years later, when I was in Congress, I would still run into old Club members and restaurant patrons on the campaign trail, who would say to me "I remember you—you're Joey the Waiter!"

I did well at Fordham University, and that led to a terrific opportunity: an internship with Arthur Andersen & Co. I was invited to join the firm in 1962 and three years later became a Certified Public Accountant. In 1972, when I was only 31, Andersen made me a full partner.

One of my professional accounting and tax specialties was charitable and other nonprofit organizations. As I learned more and more about our remarkable network of philanthropic, civic and service organizations—a feature of American life noted by visitors as far back as de Tocqueville in the 1830s—I was struck at how widespread the idea was of a successful individual giving something back to the community in which he had prospered. It was not, as I had thought, merely a notion that Dad and Mom had implanted in me, but something truly American, common not only to poor immigrants who had made good, but to millions of other citizens who in their own way worked to improve their communities and ameliorate their country's ills.

So in addition to my professional responsibilities as a CPA, I got involved in all sorts of charitable, civic and community activities. These personal efforts, in addition to my professional activities, gave me a wide range of contacts and friends throughout New York City and adjacent Westchester County, where I had lived for many years.

Then in 1984 I did something many of my friends thought was akin to tilting at windmills—others, less generous, told me I was nuts. I decided to run for Congress. Why me? I had little experience with politics, and certainly was not a "politician" of any sort. I was a partner with 22 years tenure in one of the world's leading accounting firms. Run for Congress? Get serious!

The Democratic incumbent, Richard Ottinger, had been in Congress for a long time and had once run for the U.S. Senate, losing a close three-way race to James Buckley in 1970. He was well known throughout Westchester County, neither touched by scandals nor on the verge of senility, and reputedly very wealthy. But I decided to take on this local titan because I relished the challenge, and because I thought I could bring something useful and different to the Congress of the United States—the perspective of an ordinary citizen and CPA, someone who could understand what actually happened in the towns and villages of Westchester when Congress made some high-blown pronouncement down there inside the famous Washington Beltway. I may not have known much about politics, I thought, but I was confident that I knew the territory and could understand the numbers.

Maybe this was a crazy idea—but my penniless dad had had a crazy idea too. He dreamed of owning his own grocery store, and with hard work and sacrifice he and my mom made it come true. So I was raised to be a "possibility thinker," subscribing to the ten most powerful two-letter words in the English language: "If it is to be, it is up to me." Anyway, no one else seemed interested in tackling Congressman Ottinger.

So I started learning about how to be a candidate for Congress, and I began raising funds from those I had worked with in all those professional, charitable and civic activities over the years. Many generously volunteered time and money, but I suspect that in their hearts they thought I was at least marginally off my rocker.

Then, the unexpected happened: Congressman Ottinger decided not to seek re-election. Suddenly Republican primary candidates popped up all over the place. These "would-be congressmen" had been hiding out in the tall grass while Dick Ottinger was a candidate. Now they were saying, "Don't waste time with DioGuardi. He's a good guy, but a total amateur. What does he know about getting elected? And what would he do as a naive freshman congressman? Vote for *me!*"

That line sounded pretty convincing. But it didn't work.

I persisted in my crusade as the "common-sense" candidate. People throughout my district responded by saying, "So, Joe's just an accountant. But he's competent. He's honest. He's dedicated. He's done a world of good for our community. He was willing to go out and tackle Dick Ottinger while the rest of you were waiting for someone to hand you something on a silver platter. I'm sticking with Joe."

By the time of the Republican convention in June, all the other Republican aspirants had dropped out of the running. I won the nomination and then, five months later, defeated Congressman Ottinger's protégé, who had become the Democratic candidate after a bruising four-man primary contest.

"Joey the Waiter" was suddenly a member of the Congress of the United States, with a vote (on the floor, at least) every bit as potent as that of Tip O'Neill, Jim Wright, Dan Rostenkowski, Bob Michel, Newt Gingrich, Jack Kemp and many other famous names of American politics. How proud Dad and Mom were to see their eldest son—the floor sweeper, order boy, shelf stocker, accordion player and waiter—seated in the House of Representatives of the Congress of the United States! On that wonderful day in January 1985, they, my wife, my children and I thought to ourselves: "Only in America!"

But, day by day, after the congratulations and the photographs and the ego-inflating thrill of becoming a congressman subsided, I began to learn some things about the Congress that weren't in Civics 101 at Fordham Prep.

What I found out, in a nutshell, is this: Congress deceives "we the people."

By that I don't mean that every member of Congress lies, although many of them do it often enough to make an honest man wonder whether the statue of Freedom on the Capitol Dome ought not be replaced by, say, Mercury, the god of deception.

What I mean is that, as a collective body, Congress continually, systematically and shamelessly deceives the American people by failing to disclose the true cost and financial condition of our federal government. Many members who can still tell falsehood from truth condone all this as a normal, if somewhat regrettable, practice. This book is about that practice and its implications for our democracy and the future of America itself.

I was brought up to understand that dishonesty, whether by acts committed or omitted, is not only morally wrong, but also leads to unhappy consequences.

You can't shortchange customers in your grocery store and expect to stay in business on the streets of the Bronx.

You can't siphon off capital funds to pay lavish executive bonuses and expect to remain a respected charity.

You can't sell city notes backed by the real estate taxes that the owners of abandoned buildings are never going to pay.

In fact, there is no place in America where businesspeople, nonprofit organization executives or public-sector financial managers can get away with such dishonest practices for long—with one exception: the Congress of the United States.

It is my profound hope that those who read the following pages will be motivated enough, even *angry* enough, to put an end to that exception.

# Chapter One

# THE MOST EXPENSIVE CREDIT CARD IN THE WORLD

WE ACCOUNTANTS ARE famous for getting to the bottom line. So, I will give it to you straight: You owe the federal government $31,174.89. That's your share, as an average taxpayer, of the accumulated debts run up by your irresponsible Congresses.

Year after year, budget after budget, our nation's debt has been stacked up like so many junk cars. And at the bottom of it all is a morass of fiscal mismanagement, political doublespeak and postponed obligations. You may wonder: Is this the way it's supposed to work? Did the Founders' vehicle for representative government—our Congress—wind up being a lemon?

The truth is that the system, old as it is, can be effective. History tells us so. For example, from 1801 to 1817 Congress was terribly concerned about the national debt, which resulted from federal assumption of state debts, the Louisiana Purchase and the War of 1812. So, by 1817 Congress had set up a national debt retirement plan that actually worked. In December 1834, Andrew Jackson's

1

Treasury Secretary Levi Woodbury reported to Congress: "Before the close of the year, the United States will present that happy, and probably in modern times unprecedented spectacle, of a people substantially free from the smallest portion of a public debt."

Unfortunately, that happy condition lasted only a year; by the end of 1836, Congress had taken off on an irresponsible debt binge.

And they're still at it! Today, like the rest of our spendthrift society, they run up debt with what amounts to a credit card—and they go to great lengths to make sure you can't figure out the size of the bill. After all, the system has been designed and refined to meet one overriding goal: to re-elect congressmen. The less you know about what they do, the more likely you are to re-elect them. But before I explain their trick with the credit card, you'll need to understand just how Congress goes about spending your money.

The Constitution allows only those federal expenditures authorized by Congress. So Congress passes authorization bills—for one-time expenditures, expenditures for a fixed period of years, or permanent, unlimited expenditures—"such amounts as may be appropriated." For example, Congress specifically authorizes spending for bombers, battleships, food stamps, national parks and Medicare.

But authorization is only the first step. There are many things on the books that have been authorized, but upon which no funds are being spent. For example, although the National Home Ownership Foundation was authorized in the Housing Act of 1968, it was never organized and funds never were appropriated for it. To spend the money it has authorized, Congress passes annual appropriation bills. These specify the actual amounts of money to be spent on each authorized program in the coming fiscal year, which ends on the last day of September.

Following enactment of the 1990 Budget Adjustment Act, the process now works like this. In the second week of January the president sends to Congress a proposed budget for the fiscal year beginning the following October 1, nine months later. By February 15, the committees of the House and Senate must report to their respective Budget Committees how much the programs under their jurisdiction are projected to spend in the coming fiscal year, and how much the revenue laws are expected to bring in. By April 15 both houses are supposed to have completed action on the budget

2

resolution. This resolution is a guideline for the various committees of House and Senate establishing the spending ceilings and estimated revenue for the coming fiscal year. Then each of those committees is supposed to prepare an authorization package which conforms to the Budget Resolution guidelines. Later on, if Congress gets the urge to authorize extra spending or reduce projected revenues, that action is subject to a point of order, and cannot be considered on the floor of the House. By a two-thirds vote, however, the House can waive all points of order—making this rule softer than it appears.

Once all these authorization changes have been identified, they are enacted (supposedly) by June 15 through the "reconciliation bill." This bill may include tax increases as well, so that the total of tax increases and authorization cuts produces the bottom line number called for in the budget resolution. In the past fifteen years since this process was created (1976–90), Congress met the June 15 deadline eleven times. Twice it completed work only eight days late. The other two times the resolution didn't pass until August 1 and October 1.

Meanwhile, the House and Senate Appropriations Committees prepare the 13 appropriation bills, allotting the funds required to pay for the various government programs. The budget resolutions and the appropriations bills all have to be debated, amended and approved in both House (by June 30) and Senate. Then a House-Senate conference committee convenes to resolve disagreements. These sessions can be long and agonizing; in a major reconciliation bill as many as 256 of the 535 members of Congress have served on the conference committee and its subcommittees! The "conference report" they produce then has to be approved in both House and Senate.

Congress is supposed to complete all of these steps in time for the president to sign the bills into law before October 1, the beginning of the new fiscal year. What if Congress—this often happens—can't get its act together by October 1? Then some action must be taken to keep the government from shutting down for lack of appropriations. The solution is the "continuing resolution." This measure generally appropriates funds at the level of the previous fiscal year, until the actual appropriations bills can be passed and signed.

3

## CREATING A MONSTER

Last-minute efforts by Congress to avert budgetary disasters have produced absurd situations. The 1989 budget reconciliation bill was a prime example. Under the budget act, Congress was required to pass it by June 15, but failed to do so until 4:30 a.m. on the day before Thanksgiving. Congressman Chris Cox of California reported that "not a single member of the House or Senate was permitted even to read the budget reconciliation bill before the vote on final passage. It wasn't even hauled into the chamber until moments before the vote was conducted in the wee hours.

"So voluminous was this monster bill," continued Cox, "that it was hauled into the chamber in an oversized cardboard box. Its thousands of pages, which the clerk hadn't even had time to number, had to be tied together with rope, like newspapers bundled for recycling. While reading it was obviously out of the question, it's true I was permitted to walk around the box and gaze at it from several angles, and even to touch it."

No single person can grasp all of what is included in such a measure, although various staff members and legislators are familiar with their respective parts of it. In 1981 the reconciliation bill was cobbled together in such haste that it conferred immortality upon one Rita Seymour, a staff employee of the Congressional Budget Office. Her name and phone number had been written in the margin of the official copy of the bill, and Rita inadvertently was enacted into law by the Congress of the United States. She has since been repealed.

Thus does the "world's greatest deliberative body" handle the public's fiscal business.

## THE SEQUESTER

The much-touted Gramm-Rudman-Hollings "Balanced Budget and Emergency Deficit Control Act of 1985 (GRH) was intended to put the federal government on a path to a balanced budget, originally mandated for 1991. As originally passed, GRH spelled out the maximum deficit that could be accepted for each of the next five

4

fiscal years, and contained some enforcement methods, notably the sequestering (holding back) of funds when spending was over target.

As the law now stands, if Congress overspends the budget resolution, the dreaded sequester process comes into play. Within 15 days after Congress adjourns, late in the year, the president decides whether Congress has overspent to produce an expected deficit higher than the stated target. If it has, the president has to sequester—set aside—appropriations to keep the government on the revised deficit reduction schedule spelled out in the 1990 Budget Enforcement Act. That much-revised schedule now specifies that the deficit must shrink to $98 billion in fiscal year 1995—but don't bet on it!

Under GRH prior to 1991, the president was required to issue an across-the-board sequester order on August 25 if the expected deficit exceeded the target. There were, however, major exemptions from the order, notably Social Security, Medicare, Medicaid and food stamps. The existence of these exemptions openly invited Congress to increase spending in those categories and to create yet more exempt entitlement programs, which put the entire budget over target and caused a sequester for other non-exempt spending.

The 1990 act wisely changed the rules to make sequester more effective. Now there are three different limits: mandatory spending (entitlements, interest on the debt), defense spending, and non-defense discretionary spending. If Congress goes over target in any one of these categories, the sequester is applied only to that category. In addition, the exemptions were reduced.

To force some discipline on mandatory spending, now almost half of the budget, the "pay as you go" provisions of the 1990 act require that any new entitlement be offset either by increasing taxes or cutting some other entitlement.

Before 1990, Congress had a bad habit of waiting until after a single sequester "snapshot" date—when the president had to decide whether spending was on track or over target—then passing an expensive "supplemental" bill including all the spending that had been taken out of the earlier bills. This made it look like the deficit targets were being met. The new act allows only supplementals for "dire emergencies," as defined by the president, not Congress. If Congress wants to load up such a bill with more pork, as it usually does, the bill would be subject to a point of order on the floor. To defeat this point of order would require a super-majority vote—²/₃ of the House membership, or 60 senators. Even if that was attained it still would trigger the sequester for that category. (This is the president's interpretation; Congress thinks that if the president signs the bill after the rules were waived, he can't then sequester.)

The president signs the sequester order for the regular budget, if necessary, within 15 days after adjournment of the session of Congress. Thus Congress has a chance to act to avoid the coming disaster; but if it fails to act, down comes the presidential hammer.

That's the way the new process is supposed to work. **Unfortunately Congress has shown little capacity for doing even what its own law requires. Why? Because Congress hates discipline, especially in its favorite activity: spending your money.**

## RULES MADE TO BE BROKEN

The ink was hardly dry on the Budget Enforcement Act of 1990 when Congress brazenly violated one of its key provisions. The agreement had specified that the spending scorekeeping would be done by the Office of Management and Budget (OMB) in the Executive Branch. On the first day of the 102d Congress, the Democratic majority in the House adopted House rules specifying that the Congressional Budget Office (CBO), not the OMB, would keep score. Since the CBO is controlled by the Democrats, its spending estimates are invariably designed to favor what the Democrats (and, to be fair, many Republicans) want, namely, more spending.

President Bush complained that the OMB scorekeeping had been "specifically negotiated and agreed to and cannot be arbitrarily reversed," but to no avail. The vote to shift to CBO scorekeeping was 241–160, strictly on party lines. A Republican House facing a Democratic president possibly might do the same thing, but this seems an inconceivable combination on both counts.

Two months later the House struck again. Budget Committee Chairman Leon Panetta (D-CA) tried to get the House to reduce other spending to pay for increased veterans' benefits, and keep the defense appropriations bill revenue neutral, as required. The House voted that down 175–248, largely along party lines. It is evident that the reforms agreed to in November 1990 had turned out to be illusory in mid-1991. The president had been willing to stick to his end of the deal, but a majority in Congress reneged with a vengeance.

In a budget totaling well over a trillion dollars, adopted by a body with so little fiscal responsibility as your Congress, should anyone wonder why there is little effective control of public spending? For the fiscal year that ended on September 30, 1991, here were the facts of life:

- Your government spent $1.323 trillion, 24.2% of the 1990 Gross National Product ($5.465 trillion).

- Your government took in $1.054 trillion, 19.3% of the 1990 Gross National Product.

- The difference between what taxpayers paid in and what government paid out was $269 billion—the budget deficit for fiscal year 1991. This amount is added to the national debt, which is the accumulated deficit from prior years.

- The last year the federal government was able to balance its books was 1969. Since then we have had 22 unbroken years of deficits. The total of these 22 deficit years, counting "off budget" activities, was $2.419 trillion.

The "national debt" is the amount owed by the U.S. government to those who hold its notes, bills and bonds. In 1969 the national debt was $365.8 billion. By the end of fiscal year 1991 it was $3.662 trillion. (This does not include any allowance for things the government is obliged to pay for in the future, a point we'll discuss later.) Even allowing for the depreciation of the dollar between 1969 and 1991, the national debt has more than doubled.

An estimated $206.3 billion will be spent in fiscal 1992—14.2% of the total budget outlays—merely to pay the interest on this enormous accumulation of debt.

How did we get into this era of almost uncontrolled federal deficit spending? Because the American people unwittingly gave an unlimited credit card to the wrong people—their representatives in Congress.

7

## PUT IT ON THE PLASTIC

If you're like most Americans, you've been responsible with your personal finances. You've done your best to pay your bills on time. You don't live beyond your means, at least not for long, and you don't incur debts that your children will be obliged to repay later on.

Now suppose you had a charge card with no credit limit, one that sends you only one statement a year—and a confused one at that. And suppose that you weren't required to pay the balance; you could postpone payment into the next year or even the next century. What would you say? You'd probably say, like the comedian Yakov Smirnov, "What a country!"

Well, I had one of those credit cards. So did 434 other Americans. And it worked like a dream but, I'm afraid, with nightmarish consequences for the future.

"The Card" was my plastic voting card in the House of Representatives. It had my picture on it, and a bunch of coded perforations, and every time I slipped it into the electronic voting terminal on the floor of the House, things happened. If I pressed the "yes" button, a green light appeared by my name on a huge screen above the House floor. If I pressed the "no" button, a red light came on. If the vote was a quorum call, an orange light came on.

And when a majority of the members using their cards approved the conference report on a spending bill, a lot of other things began to happen—once the president added his signature. Money—your money—turned up in a Mississippi water project. The Air Force bought some new bombers. Peace Corpsmen departed for Ecuador. Cranberry researchers got more paychecks. The Washington Monument stayed open.

To most people, spending power means the American Express Gold Card, which lets you run up a bill of $5,000 before your personal spending is halted. Or the Platinum Card, which allows you and your family to spend $10,000. But those cards are nothing compared to what I call The Most Expensive Credit Card in the World—a congressman's voting card. It has no limit!

And the best part of it: Once you're a member of Congress, you never get the bill, and they don't deduct the amount of your congressional spending votes from your paycheck. Of course, you may have to spend a lot of your supporters' money to stay in Congress, but while you're there, its the closest thing to financial Easy Street there is in America today.

There is one small annoyance with The Most Expensive Credit Card in the World. It's called the debt limit or, more precisely, the Second Liberty Bond Act, which puts a ceiling on the total federal debt. But with the very same "credit card" a member can vote to raise the limit. This happens almost every year.

Nearly everyone is familiar with the American Express credit card commercial on TV—the one where a spokesman asks, "Do you know who I am?" and then extols the virtues of using the card. If that spiel isn't enough to get you to spend what you may not yet have earned, the commercial ends with the admonition, "Don't leave home without it!"

Many times before audiences I have used the same technique to educate the American people in the cause of fiscal sanity in Washington. My spiel goes something like this:

> Some people need that American Express Gold Card with its $5,000 limit to feel powerful. Others need the Platinum Card with its $10,000 limit to feel really powerful. I've got a card that puts those two to shame—my congressional voting card.

> *[here I hold up the card]*

> My friends, take a good hard look at this card. This is the Most Expensive Credit Card in the World! This card has no limit! Now when you or your spouse gets a call from American Express or Master Charge or VISA saying you've reached your credit limit, you KNOW economic reality has arrived. You might sit down with the family around the kitchen table and review your standard of living. You might even put off a vacation.

> *[holding the card up again]*

> Not with this card. Last year the national debt reached almost three trillion dollars. And what did Congress do?

> *[raising the card higher]*

9

They just raised the limit—it's called the debt ceiling. They say, "Pass it on to the kids, let them pay for it." My friends, we have a credit card mentality in Washington, and

*[pointing to card again]*

we must remove this card from those legislators, Democrat or Republican, who are using it irresponsibly. I'm Joe DioGuardi, and believe it or not, I'm the only practicing Certified Public Accountant ever elected to Congress. I want your help in putting the heat on Congress to act responsibly—because I don't want my children, or yours, to have to pay for The Most Expensive Credit Card in the World. Do you? If you agree with me, please call Truth in Government for more information. Here's my number: 914/967-7438.

Don't leave home without it!

This little bit of play acting really gets the point across. Multiply it by a thousand audiences, or a national television audience, and I think we'd start to see some real results.

MOST PEOPLE GET a monthly statement for every credit card they use. But our federal government sends you no such statement. If it did, your most recent one would look like this (see facing page): Skipping first to the bottom line, note first that you, the average taxpayer, are in hock for a staggering $31,174.89.

At the end of the previous year (fiscal 1990) you owed $28,796.75. But your friends in Washington have been using the card quite a bit, so now your personal share of our national debt has grown to $31,174.89.

As you can see, the following "purchases" were charged to your card: your individual share of Social Security, Medicare, defense, welfare and income security, farm subsidies, foreign aid, criminal justice, and a bunch of other things included in "Other," just to keep the statement manageable.

Of course, you made some payments. Between your individual income tax payments, your Social Security "contributions," and miscellaneous other taxes, tariffs, and fees, you paid in $9,325.94. Thank you for your prompt payment! Unfortunately your check failed to cover all of the "purchases" your government made in your name. And, of course, there is the ever-present finance charge, your

*The Most Expensive Credit Card in the World*

## U.S. TAXPAYER PERSONAL CREDIT CARD STATEMENT
### FISCAL YEAR 1991
(October 1, 1990–September 30, 1991)

| DESCRIPTION | CHARGES | PAYMENTS |
|---|---|---|
| **Previous Balance Due** (*your share of the national debt beginning of year*) | $28,796.75 | |
| **Purchases During Year** (*your share*) | | |
| Social Security and Medicare | 3,305.34 | |
| National Defense | 2,411.63 | |
| Income Security and Welfare | 1,514.96 | |
| Health | 629.94 | |
| Education, Training, Employment | 367.07 | |
| Agriculture, Natural Resources | 297.10 | |
| Transportation | 279.04 | |
| Administration of Justice | 108.81 | |
| Other | 1,064.42 | |
| **Payments Received During Year** (*your share*) | | |
| Individual Income Taxes | | $4,140.06 |
| (*Thank you for your prompt payment*) | | |
| Social Security taxes and contributions | | 3,504.52 |
| Other | | 1,681.36 |
| **Totals** | 9,978.31 | 9,325.94 |
| **Finance Charge** (*your share of the Interest on the national debt*) | 1,725.77 | |
| **New Balance Due** (*your share of the national debt end of year*) | $31,174.89 | |

| PREVIOUS BALANCE | PURCHASES | FINANCE CHARGES | PAYMENTS | BALANCE DUE |
|---|---|---|---|---|
| $28,796.75 | $9,978.31 | $1,725.77 | -$9,325.94 | $31,174.89 |

\* NOTE: This statement is based on the cash accounting system still used by the federal government, not the Generally Accepted Accounting Principles used by most state governments and private industry.

SOURCE: Final Monthly Statement of Receipts and Outlays of the United States Government for FY 1991 (Financial Management Service, Department of the Treasury); IRS 1991 estimate of 113 million joint and individual income taxpayers.

share of the $195 billion in interest the federal government paid to those who bought the securities the government issued in order to continue its deficit spending binge.

And so your personal bottom line is $31,174.89—your balance due.

If this scares the hell out of you, you are not alone. Congress' credit-card mentality is a tremendous threat to our prosperity and our security. **It's bad enough that you are taxed to pay for much of this spending. But an even more serious problem flows from the fact that the shortfall between congressional appropriations and your tax payments must be made up by borrowing from the public, a large share of which is now borrowed from the Japanese, British and Germans.**

If you apply for a new car loan, the bank will inquire as to how and when you intend to pay it back, and they'll put a lien on your car to secure the loan. Not so with the federal government. When it borrows to finance the deficit, it never worries about paying it back. When its bonds, notes and bills come due, the Treasury simply issues more bonds, notes and bills and uses the proceeds to redeem the old ones. This is the financial equivalent of what Ponce de Leon was looking for in the jungles of Florida—the Fountain of Youth.

What happens when the Treasury issues all of these IOUs to finance the deficit? America's investment-generating private savings are diverted into current government spending, and foreign lenders finance more and more of our deficit and national debt. Or, if the Federal Reserve System buys the IOUs from commercial banks, new money is put into circulation, the value of the dollar drops, and inflation accelerates again. Neither is a happy result.

The more Washington competes in the credit markets to finance deficits, the more interest rates are pushed up. As a result, Americans must pay more to borrow for homes, cars and other necessities. The costs of borrowing for our children's college educations increase, along with tuitions. High interest rates also make it more expensive for American business and industry to invest in new equipment and technology. In our competitive world, that often means that foreigners make and sell the products once made by Americans, increasing our trade deficit as well.

The American people are not wholly ignorant of all this. But thanks to a Congress which conceals and fudges what it is doing, and which cannot live by the laws it passes in rare moments of reform, our country is sliding into an ever-deeper hole.

You can't just eliminate or recall that unlimited "credit card" that members of Congress enjoy—it's not that easy! But you should be able, through the election process, to take individual cards away from those members who have used them irresponsibly. "We the People" can pressure Congress to fess up about what it does. You can pressure Congress to tell you the truth. You can pressure Congress to keep its financial accounts and reports in straightforward, honest form so you can hold its members accountable. **You can demand an end to the fiscal sleight of hand, the smoke and mirrors, the accounting gimmicks, and the outright duplicity of the federal budget process.**

Later in this book I'll make some suggestions as to how you, as a citizen and taxpayer, can do that. But first, so you know what you're up against, let's take a look at some of the sleazy gimmicks and practices Congress has used, and continues to use, to keep Americans in the dark (or—I should say—in the red!).

# Chapter Two

---

# PLASTIC BUDGETING

---

DAVID STOCKMAN, AT the conclusion of his four stormy years as director of the Office of Management & Budget (OMB), gave a speech to the Board of the New York Stock Exchange.

"As the fiscal crisis has worsened and the political conflict intensified," he said, "we have increasingly resorted to squaring the circle with accounting gimmicks, evasions, half-truths and downright dishonesty in our budget numbers, debate and advocacy. **Indeed, if the Securities and Exchange Commission had jurisdiction over the executive and legislative branches, many of us would be in jail.**"

A lot of things Stockman said produced strong controversy, but to my knowledge no one ever took issue with that remark. As a CPA with many years of experience in the private sector, I knew what might have happened had I tried some of the now-famous gimmicks practiced in the federal budget process: the loss of a client for my firm; the loss of my job; perhaps the loss of my license to practice. At worst, I'd be sent off to another federal operation—like Leavenworth.

To an accountant trained in a profession that demands rock-solid integrity, federal budgeting is far from rock solid. It is, metaphorically, plastic budgeting, approved by people with little plastic cards and elastic standards of fiscal integrity.

It would be an exhausting task to present an encyclopedia of the ways Congress deliberately conceals the facts and misleads the public about the budget. But, just to give you the flavor, here is a "dirty dozen" of budgeting chicanery developed over the years.

## GIMMICK 1: FUDGING THE ECONOMIC NUMBERS

When you project a federal budget for a future year, someone has to arrive at a set of crucial economic assumptions. Many federal payments, such as Social Security, are tied to the inflation rate, so first you must decide what that rate is likely to be. Since income taxes depend on corporate profits and thus on Gross National Product (GNP), you need to know how much you can reasonably expect GNP to go up (or possibly even down). Interest payments on federal debt depend on the market interest rate, so you must have some idea of what that rate is likely to be. These numbers, and others, are interrelated: move one, and they all move.

Every forecaster, including the OMB, the Treasury, and the Congressional Budget Office (CBO), has a complex computer model of government finances and the economy. If you enter one set of numbers, the model will give you a complete, consistent set of output numbers on which the budget is based. But what are the "best" numbers and assumptions to use? That depends in large part upon for whom one works. The OMB, in the Executive Office of the President, tends to generate numbers that will make the president look good—usually low inflation, high real growth, low interest rates, and a shrinking budget deficit.

Stockman, in his remarkable book *The Triumph of Politics*, tells how the Reagan Administration arrived at its economic input numbers in the spring of 1981. Competing groups of experts were haggling over the numbers. As the deadline approached for locking up the Reagan budget, Stockman called in Murray Weidenbaum, Chairman of the Council of Economic Advisers, and made a political deal. If Weidenbaum would agree to a "reasonably high" real growth rate, Stockman would accept whatever inflation rate was consistent with it.

When the "deal" was announced at the final economic meeting, there were grumbles from all of the contending factions. Finally someone turned to Weidenbaum and asked, "What model did this come from, Murray?"

"Weidenbaum," wrote Stockman, "glared at his inquisitor a moment and said, 'It came right out of here.' With that he slapped his belly with both hands. 'My visceral computer.'" And thus were determined the economic assumptions that would shape a $745 billion national budget.

Sen. Hank Brown (R-CO), then a dedicated, anti-spending congressman, launched a well-informed attack on phony economic numbers in a 1985 article. In the article he pointed out Congress' bad habit of picking economic numbers that would show the deficit shrinking—numbers wildly unattainable in the real economy.

Brown showed that using these phony numbers drastically underestimated future deficits. For example, the 1982 budget resolution forecast a $1 billion surplus for fiscal year 1984; in fact, there was a $175 billion deficit. The third-year projections of Congress were off by more than $100 billion each year from 1980 up to the time Brown wrote in 1985.

The budget resolutions of 1985, said Brown, assumed a Treasury Bill rate of 7.9% in fiscal 1986. Even as Congress offered that assumption, the financial futures markets—where actual money was being spent for Treasury Bill futures—forecast rates ranging from 8.2% to 8.9% for the same period. Concluded Brown: "It would be nice to live in a fantasy world. But reality inflicts painful lessons on those who try to ignore it. It is time for Congress to deal with deficits realistically. We can't assume them away." Amen. (By the way, Hank Brown sat for the CPA exam and passed while serving with me in the House; he was elected to the Senate in 1989.)

## GIMMICK 2: OFF-BUDGET TREATMENT

If your spending program threatens to increase the budget deficit, there is a very straightforward way of neutralizing it: Put it "off budget." A recent example of this technique lies in the operation of the Strategic Petroleum Reserve (SPR). It takes tax dollars to fill up the SPR with purchased oil, and that exacerbates the deficit. So in 1989 the Bush Administration simply declared the reserve to be off budget. That reduced the expected deficit by $3.7 billion, but the Treasury still had to go out and borrow the money to pay for the oil.

Another famous example of the off-budget scam was the Federal Financing Bank (FFB). This operation was created with good intentions in 1974 as a way to save the government money. The Bank raised funds in the marketplace for various agency programs that previously had sold their own bonds. Here's how it worked. The Farmer's Home Administration (FmHA) would make loans to farmers and rural communities. Pretty soon the agency would be "loaned out"—all its funds used up. So FmHA would sell the FFB a "Certificate of Beneficial Ownership" for the pool of loans it had made. With the proceeds of this "sale" FmHA would go out and make more loans.

Now the FFB would possess paper certificates from FmHA, but no more money. So the FFB would go out to the capital market and sell more of its bonds to raise funds for the next go-round. In 1990 the amount of FFB's outstanding loans was about $134 billion.

But because FFB was set up off budget, the net effect of this sale was the appearance that FmHA had no on-budget spending. For example, if FmHA made $5 billion of loans in a year, and sold $5 billion in certificates to the FFB, the $5 billion coming in would cancel the $5 billion going out, and FmHA's on-budget outlays would appear to be zero. The FFB would have an outlay of $5 billion—but off budget and not counted in the budget deficit. Of course, the FFB would have to go back to the Treasury and borrow billions more to start the cycle all over again.

Fortunately, this particular off-budget device is now history. A 1985 statute put the FFB back on budget, and in 1990 the Bush Administration started to sell off the FFB's assets, covering with appropriated funds the expected $700 million losses on the sales.

**The most bizarre example of the off-budget scam, according to Carol Cox of the Committee for a Responsible Federal Budget, is the one used to keep most of the 1989 savings and loan bailout off budget.** The government created a new off-budget borrowing institution, the Resolution Trust Corporation (RTC). The RTC borrows $50 billion off budget, and pays it to the on-budget (and insolvent) Federal Savings and Loan Insurance Corporation (FSLIC). According to federal government accounting, those payments become government revenue and reduce the budget deficit. The interest payable on the RTC bonds, however, are on-budget appropriations which increase the deficit. But because the payments to FSLIC will be many times the interest appropriations, the net effect will be deficit reduction.

According to Karen Diegmuller, writing in *Insight*, it is as if a husband goes to the bank and borrows $100. He gives $50 to his wife to pay a bill, and they assume they have "saved" the other $50, forgetting that they had to borrow $100 in the first place. "There isn't any real good reason to do this unless we want to hide something," says Carol Cox. For Congress, of course, that is plenty good reason.


## GIMMICK 3: THE CURRENT SERVICES BUDGET

The 1974 Budget Act requires the president to submit a "current services" budget showing what it would cost to keep the government running another year if there were no changes in policy. Congress' trick is to make a change in policy to restrain spending, then brag about a cut, when in fact the only cut is to the *projected* level of spending under existing policy.

For example, suppose the government in Year One is paying food stamp benefits to 1,000 families at the rate of $3,600 per year. Based on the economic assumptions, there will be more unemployment next year and 1,100 families will qualify under the same eligibility standards. Accordingly, the current services budget will show an increase from $3.60 million to $3.96 million. Then Congress decides to tighten the eligibility standards so only 1,050 families qualify. Lo and behold, a "cut" of $180,000 (50 × $3,600) materializes. But, in fact, government food stamp spending went *up* by $80,000 over Year One. There was no real "cut"—only a reduced rate of spending increase. You can see why President Bush has blasted "wonderland budgeting," and Chrysler Chairman Lee Iacocca has said of it, "If we did this in business, they'd lock us up."

Rep. Bill Frenzel of Minnesota, one of the most experienced and conscientious members of Congress until his retirement in 1990, fought a continual war against the "current services" scam. Says Frenzel: "A current level, common-sense baseline would allow the American people to have a better understanding of how the federal government is spending their tax dollars. Our constituents don't, and shouldn't have to, understand the arcane language of current

19

services. **The public deserves an honest budget, where doing nothing is no longer counted as a cut and increases have the same meaning as they would in any family budget.**"

## GIMMICK 4: THE MAGIC ASTERISK

The magic asterisk is probably one of the most notorious budget gimmicks, and also one of the easiest to understand. In his book David Stockman describes its invention in the crucial 1981 budget very candidly. The administration's "Chapter Two" reductions fell far short of the $130 billion needed to meet the budget target. "Bookkeeping invention thus began its wondrous works. We invented the 'magic asterisk.' If we couldn't find the savings in time— and we couldn't—we would issue an IOU. We would call it 'future savings to be identified.' It was marvelously creative. A magic asterisk item would cost negative $30 billion . . . $40 billion . . . whatever it took to get a balanced budget in 1984 after we totaled up all the individual budget cuts we'd actually approved."

That year the magic asterisk came out to equal $44 billion. Stockman relates an amusing meeting with Senate Republican leaders, during which the question was raised of how to avoid the magic asterisk—either through more taxes or spending cuts. Majority Leader Howard Baker is quoted as saying, "Gentlemen, I'm tempted to designate this $44 billion with a magic asterisk. But I won't. (pause) But come to think of it, that's our only choice. And so I will." Which, says Stockman, is how the $44 billion magic asterisk was officially baptized by the politicians.

Even though the magic asterisk has become notorious, and is fairly easy to spot, its use continues. Franklin Spinney, the in-house critic of Pentagon budget gimmicks, pointed out in 1988 that the Pentagon's five-year spending plan coined a new version of the magic asterisk, which he calls "negative money." The 1990–94 defense plan turned out to be $45 billion over President Reagan's final budget. So a new budget line was inserted that simply subtracted $45 billion from the spending estimates. This "negative money" was explained as $22 billion in as-yet-unidentified procurement reductions, plus $23 billion in savings attributable to (unspecified) superior management.

One final example: in the fiscal 1992 Budget Resolution, Congress had an irresistible urge to add $1.8 billion to certain education programs. But under the rules of budget accounting adopted in 1990, adding the $1.8 billion could trigger a sequester. The solution: the magic asterisk. Congress cheerfully added an item called "unspecified spending reductions" in the amount of $1.8 billion, thus (supposedly) bringing net spending under the budget target.

## GIMMICK 5: THE FRAUD, WASTE AND ABUSE EXCUSE

Since there are few if any defenders of fraud, waste and abuse, a member of Congress can denounce such things with impunity, and sound very good to the constituents back home. Actually achieving savings by rooting out these costly activities is a lot more difficult. For instance, in the fiscal 1982 budget, the House Budget Committee simply invented savings of $6 billion, the expected benefit from finding and eliminating the terrible threesome. Of course, nobody had the faintest idea where the fraud, waste and abuse could or would be found. Congress just declared that eliminating it would produce this amount of savings.

True, one probably can find a lot of fraud, waste and abuse in a $1.4 trillion federal budget. Unfortunately it takes money to find it. Every person who uses food stamps illegally could be caught if a federal agent tracked him to see what he does with the stamps. The cost of the investigator might even be offset by the savings from the halted fraud, but that is obviously an inefficient tradeoff. **Unless and until the perpetrators of fraud, waste and abuse feel the pangs of conscience and turn themselves in—probably the same day shrimp learn to whistle—the "fraud, waste and abuse" line item will remain as unbelievable as the magic asterisk and negative money.**

## GIMMICK 6: TRUST FUND DEFICIT MASKING

This is a dandy little scam because it produces big numbers— mainly because the biggest trust fund is Social Security. Thanks to a combination of the 1983 Social Security rescue program, which hiked payroll taxes to prevent a crash of the program, and six straight years of a high-employment wage base, Social Security is now taking in much more than it is paying out. In 1992 this surplus will be about $108 billion.

Now one of the most cherished Social Security fictions is that the trust fund balance is invested to accumulate at interest for 30 or 40 years, until it is needed to pay benefits to future retirees. As we shall see in Chapter 5, there really is no such trust fund in any meaningful sense: it is just the accounting equivalent of a large cookie jar filled with notes reading "Ma, I'll pay the missing cookies back later—honest."

But from an accounting standpoint, the Social Security trust fund ran a $74 billion surplus in fiscal year 1991. This surplus cancelled $74 billion of a $342 billion deficit in all other accounts, leaving a deficit of "only" $268 billion. The trust fund surplus has the effect of reducing the current year federal deficit by 27%.

From an economics standpoint this is not a gimmick. The net effect of the federal deficit on capital markets is $268 billion, not $342 billion, since the Treasury "borrows" the Social Security surplus before it goes out to sell notes and bonds to finance its shortfall. But to an accountant the addition of the Social Security trust fund surplus 'apples' to current deficit spending 'oranges' has the effect of "masking" the true level of current deficit spending. Were it not for the trust fund surplus, people would rightly see the federal government as much further into the deficit hole.

The 1990 Budget Enforcement Act significantly improved the budget treatment of Social Security, removing the trust fund surplus from the annual deficit calculation. The Act also included "firewall" provisions intended to make it difficult to spend the projected buildup of reserves on higher benefits. This much, at least, is progress.


## GIMMICK 7: THE GIVE-AND-TAKE

This once-famous scam is scarcely seen anymore because it was so patently ridiculous that even members of Congress were ashamed to do it.

The debt limit increase bill of 1972 contained a bold, unequivocal provision, section 201(a), which declared that not a penny more than $250 billion could be spent on federal programs in fiscal 1973. Immediately below it came section 201(b), which said that the ceiling imposed by section 201(a) would become null and void *one day* after the bill was signed into law, along with any action taken during that one day—presumably by President Nixon.

This scam reminds me of the story of the Oklahoma Democratic Party convention of many years ago, where prohibition was the hot issue. The wets and the drys fought tooth and nail, but neither had the votes to prevail without shattering the party. Finally, they reached a compromise: the party came out foursquare for a ban on the sale of alcoholic beverages, but pledged that the ban would not be enforced.

## GIMMICK 8: PHONY LIABILITY VALUATIONS

Suppose you unwisely lend your shiftless brother-in-law $5,000 to buy a used car, and soon after he skips town for Mexico. You are later asked by your bank for a net-worth statement so you can get a loan for a new home. On your statement, under "Assets," you put "Promissory note—$5,000." You know fully well you'll see neither the $5,000 nor the brother-in-law again, but you list the note anyway. As your banker or accountant would be glad to explain to you, that's fraud.

Unfortunately, Uncle Sam makes this kind of bluff all the time. For example, the Federal Deposit Insurance Corporation (FDIC), which insures your bank account to $100,000, collects premiums from banks to build up a reserve fund. Until the early 1980s this worked pretty well. Bank failures were rare, usually resulting from mistakes or fraud by individual officers.

But in the 1980s a massive contraction of agricultural land values and oil prices hit parts of the country very hard, particularly the Southwest. Banks started going under everywhere. The FDIC continued to value the loans of their insured banks at face value, even though the values obviously were plummeting. Then, suddenly, with depositors standing in line to have Uncle Sam pay them off, the truth hit: the FDIC was broke, and Congress had to put in billions of tax dollars to meet its obligations.

The same thing went on for years with Third World debts. Banks that had made loans to Argentina, Mexico and Brazil showed those loans at face value, even though the same types of loans were being sold in the secondary market at well below half their face value. For several years the government agencies regulating and protecting the banks blithely accepted the banks' false valuation of these loans, rather than face the fairly serious financial and foreign policy repercussions. In a famous—or infamous—address to the New England Council in November 1982, Fed Chairman Paul Volcker said that "where new loans facilitate the adjustment process and enable a country to strengthen its economy and service its international debt in an orderly manner, new credits should not be subject to supervisory criticism"—an open invitation to falsify asset valuation which had become common by the time the S&L industry crashed a few years later.

## GIMMICK 9: FRONT-LOADING

A favorite trick of budgeteers is to front-load a new program—collecting taxes to pay for it for a year or so before the benefits begin to be paid out. Thus for a year or two the deficit is reduced by the new revenues. Only in the later years do the program costs overwhelm the revenues and add to the deficit—but, of course, that's somebody else's problem.

In 1988 Congress passed the Medicare Catastrophic Coverage Act. Not so wisely, in retrospect, Congress levied a tax of up to $800 on senior citizens to pay for the program. The tax went into effect promptly, but the benefits weren't to be paid until later. Why? So $5 billion could be sucked in to reduce the deficit immediately. As it turned out, this particular scam backfired. The outcries of senior citizen groups forced repeal of the tax, and the entire benefit program with it, in 1989.

## GIMMICK 10: RECONCILIATION SAVINGS

Some of the most creative work ever done by Congress comes in the statements by House committees as to how they propose to meet

24

the guidelines of the first budget resolution. That resolution in effect tells each authorizing committee of the House (and Senate) to adjust its program to meet a target number. "Bald faced lying" would be too mild a term to describe the responses to this unwelcome instruction.

This is how the Armed Services Committee claimed $1 billion in "savings." Military retirement law says retirees get a twice-a-year cost-of-living (COLA) adjustments in their paychecks. But if civilian retirees were to have their twice-a-year COLA changed to once a year, military retirement payments would, by law, have to follow suit. So the Armed Services Committee "assumed" that the Civil Service Committee would go to the once-a-year COLA, as the Administration had requested. Since that change would be matched by the military retirement system, the Armed Services Committee went ahead and claimed a $1 billion "savings."

However, the Civil Service Committee, which Stockman described as "a wholly owned subsidiary of the federal employee unions," had no intention whatever of abandoning the twice-a-year COLAs for its main constituency. The Armed Services Committee members knew this well; their claim of savings was bogus.

The Civil Service Committee was even more creative. It claimed $15 billion savings over three years by putting a cap on federal civilian employee pay increases. Wonderful! But in the fine print the committee specified that the cap could not actually be imposed unless the president imposed comprehensive wage and price controls on the entire U.S. economy, something the committee knew fully well President Reagan would not do.

The House Public Works Committee dutifully came up with billions in future savings for water projects, mass transit, highways, etc. How were all these billions to be saved? The committee merely sent a formal letter to the House Budget Committee solemnly promising that it would be done! (Stockman writes that this effort won the chutzpah award.)

## GIMMICK 11: SHIFTING SPENDING TO ANOTHER YEAR

This gimmick has been around a long time and is very popular. It requires only changing the date of an expenditure to fall into a different fiscal year, so that the current fiscal year's deficit objectives are more likely to be met.

In 1989 this was done, conspicuously, in two cases. Certain farm payments due in fiscal 1990 were accelerated to fall into 1989, along with the October 1 military payday, which magically arrived on September 29. Of course, the money still had to be paid out, so why worry about shifting it from one year to another? The answer is that fiscal 1989 was already "lost"—the deficit reduction targets mandated by GRH had not been met for that year, so a larger deficit wouldn't matter. If, however, the outlays were made in fiscal 1990, they would affect whether the GRH targets were met for that year. Since the political price had already been paid for failing to meet the 1989 targets, a larger deficit cost nothing.

## GIMMICK 12: THE MONSTER BILL

The bigger and more impenetrable a spending bill is, the more likely it is to conceal lots of budgetary stinkers. As Congressman Chris Cox observed (in Chapter 1), members are not even allowed to see some of the bills they are voting on, bills so huge they come onto the House floor bundled up like old newspapers.

The 1989 reconciliation bill occupied 1,878 pages, a number determined after it had been voted on, since there wasn't time beforehand for such formalities as page numbering. Members often are forced to rely on such monster bills because they offer the only way to bring their proposals to the floor for a vote. Editorializing on this subject, the *Wall Street Journal* said: "Republicans especially want a guarantee from the House leadership that they'll get an up-or-down vote on the bills [they favor]. House Speaker Foley ought to deliver that promise. This is the way government is supposed to work, with politicians taking responsibility for votes that their constituents can identify, instead of concealing them in the great reconciliation garbage truck."

The monster bill has another vice. Once passed by Congress, the bill either can be signed or vetoed by the president—there's no middle ground. Thus Congress is fond of throwing in lots of separate provisions that the president ordinarily would veto, but can't, since he would have to veto the whole bill and shut down the government. (President Reagan actually did this in the fall of 1981.) There is increasing speculation that President Bush may declare that he has the Constitutional power to veto discrete sections of a monster bill—in effect, the line item veto. I hope he does.

## DODGING GRAMM-RUDMAN

At the time GRH was passed in 1985, even its co-sponsor Sen. Warren Rudman (R-NH) described it as "a bad idea whose time has come." So in 1990 GRH was largely supplanted by OBRA, the Omnibus Budget Reconciliation Act, which created the new budget enforcement process already described in Chapter 1.

In its three years of effective life, did GRH hold down deficit spending? Co-sponsor Sen. Ernest Hollings (D-SC) thinks not. "I want a divorce from GRH," he said in 1989, calling it now a "pure sham. . . . The 1990 budget is a deathblow to budget discipline, a spectacular jambalaya of tricks and dodges." Senate Budget Committee Chairman Jim Sasser (D-TN) says, "You keep two sets of books. The official book is based on phony savings, and then there's the real set where you leave unaddressed the problems that are getting worse." House Budget Chairman Leon Panetta (D-CA) concurs: the law "provides all the wrong incentives." Former CBO Director Alice Rivlin says "enormous efforts are being made each year to concoct a budget plan that appears to reach the next target by a combination of unrealistic optimism, shortsightedness, and outright cheating. The chances for realistic long run solutions to the budget problem have been virtually obliterated."

On the other hand, Heritage Foundation budget expert Daniel Mitchell argues that the existence of fixed GRH deficit reduction targets—even though Congress cheated on them—was instrumental in bringing the deficit down from $221 billion (1986) to the $150 billion range (1987–89). While acknowledging GRH's faults, Mitchell thinks the "floating targets" adopted in the 1990 budget deal made the abandonment of GRH a "horrible step in the wrong direction."

The major loophole in GRH—the ultimate in plastic budgeting—was its requirement that the end-of-year deficit be projected almost a year in advance. "Projections" in Washington are usually far removed from the ultimate results. All an administration has to do is "project" that spending will come in under the GRH target, and the sequester threat is gone for another year. And surprise! Every year since OMB has had the projection task, until fiscal 1990, it has projected that the targets would be met. In fiscal 1988, for instance, the projected GRH deficit target of $136 billion, certified in October 1987, turned into a $160 deficit when the smoke had cleared. No sequester.

Because the projection is all-important, every sort of scheme is employed to shrink the projected deficit in October. Social Security, though exempt from the GRH sequester penalty, was included in the GRH deficit accounting simply because it (then) produced a $74 billion surplus to offset that much deficit spending elsewhere. The Postal Service was taken out of the calculation because it is a money loser (but will undoubtedly be put back in if it ever threatens to show a profit).

The Budget Enforcement Act of 1990, part of OBRA, changed the rules for the better, but there is still plenty of room for plastic budgeting. For example, as reported by the ever-watchful columnist M. Stanton Evans, "the 1990 Act allows additional outlays and further deficits resulting from 'technical' and 'economic' revisions—which is exactly where these colossal [budget projection] errors are coming from."

One may hope for better, but even the 1990 reforms may well disappear like GRH into a morass of dishonest accounting gimmicks. **Until the day arrives when the people demand that their Congress live by honest accounting, and signs the deal in blood, plastic budgeting will continue—while our nation's prosperity and security slip down the tube.**

# Chapter Three

---

# OUR NO-ACCOUNT
# FEDERAL GOVERNMENT

---

IT'S PRETTY HARD to know where you are going if you don't know where you are. Exploring the financial management of the United States government is very much like being blindfolded and lost in the New York subway system; you don't know where you are, have no idea where you are going—and you could fall off the edge at any moment with very unpleasant results.

Many years ago President Jefferson recognized this very problem. In 1802 he wrote his Treasury Secretary Albert Gallatin:

> I think it an object of great importance . . . to simplify our system of finance, and to bring it within the comprehension of every member of Congress . . . the whole system [has been] involved in impenetrable fog. There is a point . . . on which I should wish to keep my eye . . . a simplification of the form of accounts . . . so as to bring everything to a single center; we might hope to see the finances of the Union as clear and intelligible as a merchant's books, so that every member of Congress, and every man of any mind in the Union, should be able to comprehend them to investigate abuses, and consequently to control them.

If President Jefferson could worry about "impenetrable fog" in federal financial management in 1802, imagine what he would say today!

To understand just how far we have strayed from the path of honest accounting, it's necessary to understand clearly what accountants do. In the private sector, accountants take stock of the operations of business firms so that their owners and managers will have some idea of how well they're doing. No intelligent business person wants to wake up to find that, for example, the machinery is all worn out and there are no funds to replace it, or that employees have been pocketing income unnoticed for the past ten years.

The accounting profession is very rigorous. The standards are high—they have to be high, because people place great trust in accountants. A survey commissioned by the American Institute of Certified Public Accountants in 1987, on its centennial, revealed that of a dozen leading professions, the public had the highest opinion of accountants. (The lowest? No surprise: "Members of Congress.") Accountants who "cheat"—lie, cover up, or invent bizarre treatments for a financial irregularity—will be called before a disciplinary board. They may lose their licenses to practice, be fined, or even be sent to jail. Bear in mind that this is not for stealing, but simply for failing to report stealing properly, for engaging in other dishonest practices, or for committing acts of gross negligence. Any sort of suspicion about an accountant's integrity can be fatal to continued practice. It is hard to imagine a profession whose members more jealously guard their reputations for integrity.

"Certified Public Accountant" is a title held by those accountants, and firms of accountants, who have met the highest possible standards for professional competence and integrity. In an economy where trillions of dollars are invested in the stocks and bonds of corporations about which the investor customarily has little direct knowledge, the annual reviews of independent CPAs are indispensable to investor confidence. Every corporation, partnership, trust, estate, proprietorship or nonprofit organization of any consequence requires a regular, independent audit of its books.

## BRIDGING THE GAAP

When accountants examine the books and records of a business, they apply something called "Generally Accepted Accounting Principles" (GAAP). These standards can be very complicated to apply in practice, and much of the intensive training taken by accountants is directed toward understanding how to apply them to particular businesses and industries. But, stripped of all its complications, GAAP is the application of common sense to the description of a firm's economic reality. **The goal is to tell the owners and investors—and the tax collector—how the firm is doing and how it can be expected to perform in the future.**

Any intelligent person can easily grasp the ideas behind GAAP. For instance, you must account for all the cash that comes in and goes out. If your firm orders a thousand widgets, funds must be allocated to pay the bill from the supplier when it arrives. Costs of producing various products have to be assigned to those products. Income tax withholding from employee paychecks has to be deposited in a tax account for the IRS. Illegal diversion of funds ought to show up in the accounting reports as, for example, unexpected shortfalls in revenues. Perhaps most important, the predicted cost of your promises to pay in the future must be reported and accumulated in time for payment. The two most important documents produced by an accountant are the firm's "profit and loss statement," showing whether it is making or losing money on its current operations, and its "net worth statement" or "balance sheet," which is a snapshot at a given time of what the business is worth—its assets minus its liabilities.

Accounting is more than bookkeeping, although bookkeeping is at the heart of it. Modern accounting must also deal with the complexities of the laws governing the organization, and particularly the tax consequences of various practices. The modern accountant is a far cry from Ebenezer Scrooge's Bob Cratchit, sitting on a high stool and laboring with a quill pen. He or she is now bookkeeper, informal legal advisor, tax manager, merger and acquisitions consultant, labor negotiation advisor, financial detective, management psychologist and even public relations advisor.

Accounting for the federal government is a particularly difficult business, and has been the subject of much controversy within the profession. With its power to change all the rules governing its own operation and, in effect, print new money through the Federal Reserve System, it is far different from even such a large government as that of the state of California, which must live within federal rules.

Unfortunately, the accounting of federal government financial performance is in a stage that most large businesses and many city and state governments passed through many years ago. There are several reasons for that, but a major one is this: unlike the owners of a private business, who must know the status of their firm or face failure, the "directors" of the federal government—the members of Congress—would prefer that their fiscal handiwork remain concealed. The less the public understands of the financial condition of the federal government, the easier it is for Congress to go on with its long-running campaign of irresponsible deficit spending, deferred liabilities, false projections, and budget gimmicks.

A prime example of this blinders-on approach is the government's continued use of cash accounting, which looks at what cash comes in and goes out during a particular fiscal year. What comes in are taxes, tariff revenues, user fees, asset sales proceeds, and so on; what goes out are payments to employees, contractors, landlords, vendors, bondholders, retirees, poor and not-so-poor people, and so on. The difference is the annual budget deficit. (It could also be a budget surplus, but the last one of those occurred in 1969 and there is no likelihood of another one in this century.)

## THE ACCRUAL ALTERNATIVE

The alternative to cash accounting is called accrual accounting. Under accrual accounting, all "economic events" are included as they occur, whether or not the cash actually changes hands. If someone contracts to buy a firm's widgets next year, and is likely to follow through when the time comes, that future sale becomes an economic event and should appear in the firm's financial records. By the same token, if your firm owes its employees payroll checks on the final day of the fiscal year, and doesn't pay them, that liability still remains under accrual accounting and must appear on the year-end financial statement.

Take another example: buying an aircraft carrier. Under cash accounting, the payments made to the shipyard are shown as outlays. Over the four or five years it takes to build the carrier, there are large capital cost outlays. Then over the 25 years the carrier is in service with the fleet there are no outlays for its capital cost. In effect, the capital cost has been front-loaded, although the useful life goes on far into the future. Under accrual accounting, the capital cost of the carrier is spread over its useful life, even though the cash payments are actually made during its construction period.

The virtues of GAAP-basis accrual accounting are numerous. It recognizes obligations incurred even though not yet paid. It spreads capital costs over the useful lifetime of assets. It relates asset sales to useful remaining life. It rules out the clever smoke-and-mirrors tricks that Congress uses to mask the economic reality in a given budget year. Above all, it makes fiscal responsibility and financial accountability possible.

What is really interesting here is that the federal government is legally on an accrual accounting system. The law was solemnly passed by Congress in 1950 to carry out the recommendations of the two Hoover Commissions on government management. President Truman probably gave out pens he used to sign the act that would bring in a new era of accounting sanity to Washington. Unfortunately, once the photo opportunity was over, the federal government simply ignored the law; for over 40 years since the law was passed, it has stayed on a cash accounting system, and there appear to be no legal means to make it do what Congress decreed. For what it's worth, Congress also, in 1979, solemnly passed the Byrd-Grassley amendment, which states that by 1981 the United States government shall balance its budget. How well did Congress observe this law? As the late Sen. Everett Dirksen might have said, "Ha, ha, ha and, I might add, ho, ho, ho."

My old accounting firm, Arthur Andersen & Co., has been a pioneer in promoting the adoption of accrual accounting by Washington. Back in 1975, simply as a contribution to public dialogue, Andersen prepared prototype consolidated financial statements for the federal government using, as closely as they could, GAAP. At that time the Treasury stated that our national debt was $344 billion—the sum of all the outstanding government bonds, notes and bills. In fact, Andersen found, the national debt was at least $814 billion.

When Andersen did the books on a GAAP basis again, for 1984, the "official" national debt had mushroomed to $1.3 trillion, and the true GAAP debt to an astounding $3.8 trillion. Maybe there is some consolation in the fact that Washington is now reporting a higher percentage of the true national debt than a decade ago, but the trillion-and-a-half-dollar difference is not much cause for celebration. Even the higher GAAP figure is certainly understated.

As Andersen observes, a full accounting of future liabilities for Social Security benefits would expand the GAAP debt to $6.1 trillion. This is about $25,000 for every man, woman and child in the United States today. **Andersen's report dryly notes that the GAAP-basis deficit, including the costs of future retirement liabilities, "exceeded all personal savings of the American people in 1984."**

The Financial Management Service of the Treasury Department now publishes a "prototype" consolidated financial statement for the government. Its fiscal 1988 statement reported real progress in getting all agencies to conform to a standard system. Sixteen agencies were by then on the standardized system, using accrual basis data. On October 10, 1990, OMB, the Treasury, and the General Accounting Office (GAO) signed an important Memorandum of Understanding establishing a Federal Accounting Standards Advisory Board (FASAB). With this action the federal government may well be within two or three years of establishing, at long last, a consistent accounting system that will permit a truly accurate annual statement.

## THINKING AHEAD

Capital budgeting and accounting go hand in hand with GAAP. As noted in the example of the aircraft carrier, sound reporting should spread the cost of such an asset over the years it is available for use. Historically, this has not been done. In the last three years, however, some government agencies, including Defense, have begun to treat new capital assets in accordance with GAAP principles. Congressman Bill Clinger of Pennsylvania has been an effective advocate of sound capital budgeting, and his persistent efforts seem to be bearing fruit.

A now-notorious fiscal crisis, directly attributable to bad accounting practices, stems from the condition of the nation's nuclear weapons producing facilities, such as Hanford, Rocky Flats and Oak Ridge. These giant facilities were built in the 1940s and 1950s, and paid for in those decades. Aside from maintenance and relatively minor expansions, they hummed along for forty years, all the while getting older, more decrepit, and more dangerous to their workers and, possibly, the public. All of a sudden, in 1989, the Department of Energy found out that an enormous sum—up to $150 billion, by some calculations—would have to be spent rapidly to restore these plants to safe and efficient operation. Had these assets been accounted for by a major chemical company, their deterioration and replacement would have been provided for, beginning the first day they went into operation.

Because of the cash accounting system used in Washington, there is a bias against capital investment. A new aircraft carrier or nuclear weapons facility may last forty years, but in the cash budget it appears as an outlay only during the years it's being built. Of course, the later years come "cost free," but most politicians are worried about the cash impact *now*—and that means in this year's budget. So it is politically easier to defer big chunks of capital projects (and even maintenance) until some later year, when it becomes somebody else's fiscal problem. That brings down this year's deficit. But if the project were accounted for over its useful life, the first-year costs would not be nearly as high, and thus the new investment might be affordable after all. Each investment ought to pass muster on its merits in competition.

In October 1989 Charles A. Bowsher, the Comptroller General of the United States and a highly respected accounting professional, released a GAO Report called "Managing the Cost of Government." This landmark document ought to be digested by every member of Congress, for it points the way to the kind of accounting sanity that has so long been absent from federal accounts. Bowsher's key recommendation focuses on three different kinds of spending engaged in by the federal government: general funds, trust funds and "enterprise" funds. These latter funds are entities like the Postal Service and the Tennessee Valley Authority. They provide services to the public and charge fees to the public. They also require business-type flexibility in their operations so that they can meet changes in customer demand.

Trust funds are, notably, Social Security retirement and Medicare funds, and the civil service and military retirement trust funds. During the 1980s steps were taken to change these funds from a pay-as-you-go basis, with no buildup of assets, into asset-holding funds which would be better prepared to meet large future obligations, especially when the Baby Boom generation starts to retire in about 2012. These four funds alone showed a surplus of $86 billion in 1988, and in a few years this number will escalate radically. The expected 1994 surplus of the Social Security fund alone is projected at $113 billion.

The general funds of the government comprise everything else, including domestic and defense spending, environmental protection, welfare, justice, housing and national parks. The unified budget idea, first adopted in 1969, simply adds the pluses and minuses of all three types of spending into one budget deficit number. And it is on this number that the provisions of the Budget Enforcement Act operate.

As Bowsher shows, adding these dissimilar types of spending together gives a wholly misleading picture of the financial position of the U.S. government:

| FISCAL YEAR 1988 | BUDGET RESULTS | DOLLARS IN BILLIONS | | | |
|---|---|---|---|---|---|
| | | TOTAL | GENERAL | TRUST | ENTER-PRISE |
| Restructured according to GAO Proposal (approximations) | Operating surplus or deficit | $−131 | −248 | 124 | −7 |
| | Capital Financing Requirements | −24 | −23 | 2 | −3 |
| | Unified Budget Financing Requirements | −155 | −271 | 126 | −10 |

The chart tells us that the trust funds in fiscal 1988 produced a fat surplus of $126 billion. The enterprises came in at −$10 billion, and the remainder of government operated −$271 billion in the red. The net total is the actual $155 billion fiscal 1988 budget deficit.

The trust funds, mostly Social Security, are generating a huge net surplus—on the order of $100 billion a year—which has the effect of masking a like amount of current deficit spending. But the Social Security and other retirement funds are by law pledged to cover future retirement costs of millions of Americans. **To snatch these funds and spend them to reduce the general government deficit is nothing less than a breach of fiduciary duty which no private sector accountant could accept for a minute.**

In addition, by including the enterprise accounts in the unified budget those enterprises are often shackled in their business-type operations, their efficiency made subservient to the overall need to reduce the deficit. For example, the Postal Service was recently required to reduce its hours of window service in local post offices to contribute more to deficit reduction. The repercussions of poorer service on customers are not taken into account in this calculation.

Bowsher also proposes the introduction of capital budgeting into the federal budget process. At least 37 states use a capital budget, which recognizes that certain public investments yield a stream of benefits over a long period of time and should be paid for over the same period by those who enjoy the benefits (in this case, the taxpayers). To use a private sector example, it would be silly for a college to raise tuition by $500 per each of 10,000 students to pay for a new $5 million recreation facility—all in the year it was built. Those who paid the $500 that one year would get, at most, four years of use of the facility, while future students would, in effect, get to use it free for many years. The correct treatment, of course, would be to bond for the $5 million over, say, twenty years, and let the student tuition fees pay off the principal and interest each year.

Bowsher's proposal would also depreciate government assets over their useful life, to give an indication of how fast such assets were wearing out. He advocates new controls over non-cash transactions, where the government buys things by swapping other things for them. Since these are not cash transactions, they now operate outside normal budgetary controls. An example would be the payment-in-kind program to subsidize agricultural exports, where exporters are given rice or wheat from government stockpiles which they can then sell on the private market for cash.

GOVERNMENT CREDIT PROGRAMS are particularly troublesome. Suppose the government guarantees repayment of a home mortgage. For the first few years there is essentially no budget cost to the government for this guarantee. It is an unfunded promise. If there is a mortgage subsidy involved, the subsidy amount turns up in the budget, but there is no entry for possible default of the mortgage and claims for payment against the federal government. GAO recommends that funds to cover expected repayment defaults be appropriated at the time a loan or guarantee is issued, rather than appearing later, when actual defaults happen.

Every car owner understands this principle. The car may run fine for years, but you know that one day you will be facing major engine work, rusted rocker panels, bald tires and bad brakes. The trick is to anticipate these calamities and trade your car in on a newer one at the right time—preferably just before all these things start to go wrong. If you're smart, you'll be setting money aside for a year or so before that time, so you can afford the new vehicle. Unfortunately, as so often happens, your government is not as smart as you are.

But adopting Comptroller General Bowsher's sensible recommendations for budget treatment are not enough to straighten out our "no-account" federal government. **We also need to create a working system of expert, professionally trained financial managers throughout the government, using the same high standards as their counterparts in the private sector.**

## BRINGING SANITY TO THE SYSTEM

When I was in the Congress I did an unusual thing. Whenever I could find the time, I took an Inspector General or senior government accountant or auditor to lunch. Most of them had never been asked to lunch by a congressman before. Even though I was a junior member of the minority party, they were pleased to accept my invitation, probably on the theory that it was the best they were going to get.

When I got an Inspector General's attention, I peppered him with questions about the workings of his agency, and about the internal methods used for keeping track of performance and spending. Once they got comfortable with me, they poured out some fascinating—sometimes depressing—stories of mismanagement and even scandal.

Out of those conversations, and with the counsel of many of my former partners and colleagues in the accounting profession, came a bill called the "Federal Financial Management Improvement Act." I probably should have called it something like the "Sex in Government Act"—it would have gotten more attention. Despite the crucial importance of honest and thorough accounting and financial management in our trillion-dollar government operation, most members of Congress turn glassy-eyed when someone brings up this subject, just as you might when your doctor begins discussing the medulla oblongata or your lawyer mutters about the doctrine of sic utere tuo.

The Federal Financial Management Improvement Act proposed the creation of an independent Office of the Chief Financial Officer (CFO) within the Executive Office of the President. The appointee in this office would have the power, derived from the president, to whip the financial management practices of the many federal agencies into shape and consistency. The act would create an Assistant Secretary for Financial Management within each agency to spearhead the reforms and accountability procedures established by a Federal Financial Management Council, which would be composed of all the Assistant Secretaries and chaired by the Chief Financial Officer.

Even though the act did not pass initially, some of its provisions were achieved by Executive Order. A Chief Financial Officers' Council, composed of the CFOs from all agencies that have them, began to meet in 1989, chaired by the OMB Associate Director for Management. And the 25 Inspectors General also come together to participate in the President's Council on Integrity and Efficiency, chaired by the OMB Deputy Director.

The legislative breakthrough came in late 1990, spearheaded by two of my former colleagues on the House Government Operations Committee, Chairman John Conyers (D-MI) and ranking Minority Member Frank Horton (R-NY). Passage of the Chief Financial Officers' Act of 1990 was a giant step forward for sound financial management. As passed, the bill created a Deputy Director of OMB for Management and a Controller to head a new office of Federal Financial Management within OMB. The act created CFOs in the 14 departments, the Environmental Protection Agency, and NASA, and the heads of lesser agencies are required to appoint CFOs. The act requires financial plans and status reports from all the covered agencies and—at last—spells out a strategy for producing audited financial status reports.

I naturally was sorry not to have been able to take part in final passage of these important provisions, but I was tremendously pleased to receive a nice letter from President Bush after the signing. He wrote:

> I suppose that everyone who has worked on the issue of Federal financial management improvement recalls how hard you worked,

starting back in 1986, to persuade Congress that the steps authorized by H.R. 5687 were badly needed. As a Certified Public Accountant you understood the need to strengthen the systems that provide the President, the Congress, and the American people with the information necessary to make informed decisions about how public funds are spent.

Now, Joe, your hard work has been vindicated by passage of the CFO Act by the House and Senate, and by its being signed into law. I regret only that you were not in the House to take part first hand in the ultimate passage of this important piece of legislation.

Government Operations Committee Chairman John Conyers was thoughtful enough to send me a handwritten note, saying, "It may never have happened without you." It was heartening to me to realize, once again, what my parents explained to me when I was a small boy on the streets of New York: that sometimes when you think you've lost, your efforts may lead to success in the long run.

In all honesty, however, I believe that the CFO Act, important as it is, has one significant flaw. I strongly believe that the nation's Chief Financial Officer ought to be within the Executive Office of the President, not within OMB—especially not two layers deep in OMB. The latter's primary concern is the budget and, as such, it must constantly resist the spending tendencies of the agencies. It wrangles with them over their spending plans, their statutory authorizations, and what are called "pass-backs" (annual OMB revisions of their spending requests). This unavoidable wrangling sometimes spills over into the Oval Office itself.

My concern is that by locating the CFO under a Director of OMB, the director is given a "financial management card" to play in these negotiations. That is, the director might be tempted to use the threat of an unfavorable financial management report against an agency head to try to get him or her to back down from a budget request. In my view, the CFO should have been given complete independence from the budget battles, and left to report to the president on financial management matters much as the president's Science Advisor reports to him on scientific matters. Time will tell if this concern is warranted.

Believe it or not, within six months of the CFO Act's passage, some members in Congress awoke to the possibility that sound financial management controls in the agencies might disrupt what one might delicately call long-standing bilateral arrangements beneficial to certain congressional interests. Rep. Jamie Whitten (D-MS), Chairman of the Appropriations Committee, announced in a letter to Conyers and Horton that his committee would add language to all appropriations bills for fiscal 1992 which would prohibit use of any funds to implement the CFO Act in the respective agencies.

The reason behind the Whitten letter was apparently a proposed reorganization of the Department of Agriculture's management office to comply with the CFO Act. The proposal (later modified) would have diminished the influence of a senior career employee who had been, shall we say, extraordinarily responsive to the concerns of Congressman Whitten over the years. When word of the Whitten letter and amendment got out, Conyers, Horton, OMB Executive Associate Director Frank Hodsoll, and a coalition of citizen groups spearheaded by Thomas Schatz of Citizens Against Government Waste organized to defend the CFO Act. The issue came to a head on the House floor on June 18, when the Conyers-Horton amendment to delete the Whitten amendment was approved on a vote of 341–52. One may hope that this resounding defense of the CFO Act will discourage future congressional attempts to go back to sloppy, but politically advantageous, financial management practices.

It might appear that these new steps are just addressing problems by creating more government, more units, more bureaucrats. I am sensitive to that concern, because I share the view that government is getting far too big for the capacity of the American people to support or tolerate. But, on closer inspection, the idea makes sense to anyone trained in accounting and financial management. To me, after 22 years with a Big Eight accounting firm, it is obvious that all kinds of decisions are being made badly, with millions and perhaps billions of dollars being wasted simply because there is no effective way to measure spending and performance. Worst of all, the American people are constantly being engulfed in the modern equivalent of Mr. Jefferson's "impenetrable fog." If there was a magic bullet that would end this problem, I would be the first to call for it. Unfortunately, there is not.

**The only way to correct these nagging and costly problems is to, first, summon the political will to declare that it must be done, and, second, put in place rigorous accounting and financial manage-**

ment standards, agency by agency, through a coordinated effort of experienced, dedicated professionals strongly backed up by the Executive Office of the President. Such a structure would, I am convinced, pay for itself thousands of times over. An undisciplined, no-account federal government is far too costly and inefficient for taxpayers to tolerate one minute longer.

# Chapter Four

# THE BIG APPLE AND WASHINGTON—ONE BAILOUT AFTER ANOTHER

CERTAINLY NO BANKRUPTCY in American history has ever had the impact of the collapse in 1975 of the "Big Apple"—New York City. And the curious thing about the city's fiscal collapse was that hardly anyone saw it coming.

To be sure, lots of practices in New York municipal government raised red flags. The city had agreed to very generous wage and fringe benefit provisions in contracts with its municipal unions. Its welfare system seemed to lack the capacity to say "no" to applicants who by any reasonable standard were not entitled to public support. The City University handed out free tuition to any resident who wanted it. Indeed, in 1965, ten years before the crash, Mayor Robert Wagner announced in his budget message, "I do not propose to permit our fiscal problems to set the limits of our commitments to meet the essential needs of the people of the city."

Most critics did little more than grumble about the high taxes needed to feed this system. They didn't think New York was broke.

43

But it was. Why didn't anyone figure it out? Because New York City's books were a shambles. Even where they hadn't been rigged to give false impressions, they were so utterly disorganized that even a world-class accountant would have had a hard time making out what the city was doing with its money.

Journalist Chris Welles, writing at the time in *New York Magazine*, summed it up this way:

> Accounting trickery evolved into a refined art at City Hall. The techniques were abstruse and varied. But basically, most involved time warps—specifically, pretending that expenses the city was incurring now actually wouldn't be incurred until later and that revenues the city expected to receive later had already been received. . . . Like other accounting gimmicks, this, of course, produced no new actual cash for the city, only the appearance of same. . . . Over the years, the period and extent of anticipation had grown, and the city had mortgaged itself further and further into the future. The city had also been selling notes in anticipation of income it knew might never arrive at all.

Ken Auletta, who graphically described New York's collapse in his book *The Streets Were Paved With Gold*, described "the rollovers, false revenue estimates and plain lies that have robbed taxpayers of literally billions through excessive borrowing to cover up excessive fraud," and concluded that "people have gone to jail for less." It might be noted that, at one point, Auletta himself contributed to the problem. When he ran the city's off-track betting operation in 1971, he pegged its expected 1972 profits at $25 million until his bosses arbitrarily raised the figure to $50 million. (The true receipts were $14 million.)

Martin Mayer, author of a best-selling book on banking, *The Bankers*, later wrote: "On the simplest level, the story of New York's financial collapse is the tale of a Ponzi scheme in municipal paper— the regular and increasing issuance of notes to be paid off not by future taxes or revenue certified to be available for that purpose, but by the sale of future notes. Like all chain-letter swindles, Ponzi games self-destruct when the seller runs out of suckers, as New York did in 1975."

Describing the city's use of revenue, tax and bond anticipation notes—known as RANs, TANs, and BANs—James Ring Adams wrote in *Secrets of the Tax Revolt*:

RAN-TAN-BAN. It sounded like an Aramaic incantation, and it had the magical property of making a deficit vanish. Wisely used, these notes are relatively routine but [Mayor John V.] Lindsay, like the Sorcerer's Apprentice, made them multiply beyond control. New York City resorted to selling TANs and RANs to raise money whether or not it would be getting any taxes or grants to pay them off. When the money to back the notes failed to come through, the city sold new notes to pay off the old ones, and also to cover additional hidden deficits. When the 1970–71 budget had run its course, New York City was rolling over more than $1 billion in RANs above and beyond its openly acknowledged deficit borrowing, which was handled by an issue of "budget notes."

This sum was the approximate amount of its still-growing subterranean debt.

Treasury Secretary William E. Simon, who finally emerged as the much-battered hero of New York City's recovery, recounted his first exposure to the Big Apple collapse in his splendid book *A Time for Truth*:

> Simultaneously we were seeking at Treasury to establish whether the Federal government could be of assistance. But for this we needed facts—facts about the city's expenses and obligations, facts about its revenue sources, facts about its debt structure. It was a severe shock to all of us when we found that no such facts were then obtainable. No one in New York could provide us with a document that set forth the income and expenses of the city, its assets and liabilities. We soon became enmeshed in the city's Byzantine accounts and realized that after years of tortuous accounting practices, no living human actually knew the facts we were seeking.

New York's banks had loaned the city almost $2 billion. These banks—Chase Manhattan, Citibank, J.P. Morgan & Co.—were then the giants of the world (the Japanese now have supplanted them). Their leaders were financial statesmen, like David Rockefeller, Walter Wriston and Pat Patterson. How did their banks get taken in by this, and keep on lending and lending until that awful day when bond and note buyers ran away from New York paper? **They foolishly believed what the New York City accounting system told them and other investors.** Until the eve of the collapse (late in

1974) they never thought to go behind the official—and false—statements.

The New York City collapse had something of a happy ending— thanks largely to William Simon. Many of the policies that produced the 1975 disaster are relatively unchanged, but there is one great difference: the bogus accounting and poor financial management practices have been completely reformed. The city may still waste the taxpayers' money, but no longer can it hide that fact from the taxpayers, creditors, and state and federal governments. The city that in 1975 didn't even know how many employees it had, now has four-year projections of staffing levels, borrowing and cash flows. It has a carefully policed ten-year plan for capital investments. It has what some financial writers call "one of the best management information systems among large American cities (which) rivals the practices of well-managed private firms." New York's finances are overseen not only by a beefed-up, nonpartisan Comptroller's Office, with sophisticated accounting, information and internal control systems, but also by the Municipal Assistance Corporation ("Big Mac"), the New York State Comptroller, and the city's Emergency Financial Control Board. With these systems in place it has become unlikely, in the eyes of most observers, that false or misleading financial information will be a factor in any future New York City fiscal calamity. Indeed, though in 1991 the city was again in fiscal crisis (and looking for other taxpayers to shoulder the burden), this time the problem was not bad accounting or garbled information, but political unwillingness to make realistic spending decisions. Unlike in 1975, the city now can see where the money is going; it just can't seem to stop sending it there.

## WHOSE DEFAULT IS IT?

**Congress and the Treasury, as a condition of bailing out New York in 1975, imposed rigorous public accounting and reporting standards on the city—but they are a lot less willing to impose the same tough standards on themselves.** So while New York City behaves under the scrutiny of half a dozen supervisory bodies, Congress continues its fiscal mischief and lives up to its credo: "Do as I say, not as I do."

Consider the federal government's loan guarantee and insurance programs. What do these programs "cost" the taxpayers? Even a skilled accountant couldn't easily answer that. The fiscal 1991 budget document came up with a figure of $2.844 trillion. Add to that $2.927 trillion in deposit insurance, and the number swells to $5.771 trillion. This represents a 229% growth in program spending since 1970, corrected for inflation. Even New York would blush at an increase like that.

A typical government loan program, such as that of the Small Business Administration (SBA), will lend funds directly to a small business person. To qualify, the applicant must be unable to get a private loan, presumably because the business is too risky; or an available private loan must carry such a high rate, to reflect the risk, that the business plan becomes unworkable. Thus SBA steps in with a below-market interest rate loan.

Suppose the loan is for $100,000 at a six percent interest rate. The SBA disburses the $100,000 from its funds and the full value of the loan is shown as an asset, even though a significant number of loans are never repaid. If the SBA sold off all its loans, it certainly would not get face value for the portfolio. The market would discount the loans not only because the interest rate is below market, but also because investors know that some loans will go sour and never be repaid. Still, the SBA values its outstanding loans at face value until they go bad.

Compare this with New York's practice of issuing tax anticipation notes. Cities customarily borrow funds to finance operations until once-a-year property taxes are paid. The notes sold then are redeemed a few months later, when the property tax payments come in. New York had the dubious idea of selling these notes representing taxes receivable on long-abandoned, burned-out slums. Of course, the revenues never came in—so New York merely refinanced the tax anticipation notes over and over.

New York in effect valued a non-existent real estate base as if it would produce taxes, which it would not. SBA values its portfolio as if it will produce the expected stream of repayments, which it will not. Is there some meaningful difference here?

From a fiscal responsibility standpoint, federal loan guarantees present an even greater danger. With direct loans, Uncle Sam must produce the loan amount at the outset, in real money. And the good news is that the direct loans outstanding have fallen to $162 billion and will probably keep going down.

The bad news, however, is that federal loan guarantees are going up. In 1990 the volume came to $630 billion, up from $410 billion in 1985. There is a reason for this: Not only do federal loan guarantees—for worthwhile things such as college student tuition—enjoy considerable popularity, but they are also perceived by Congress to be "free." They are not calculated in the budget limits or sequester triggers. It costs an agency nothing to guarantee all sorts of repayments in the future. The guarantee, which is now, only assures that Uncle Sam (that is, the taxpayers) will pay if things go bad. The default, which is later, makes Uncle Sam pay the bill in real money. The funds to cover the default loss are on budget, to be sure, but the guarantee which required the payment never appeared in the budget as a cost. This device is common in housing mortgage loans, farm commodity export sales, industrial export sales, foreign arms sales and college student loans (over $8 billion of which are now being paid by the government because it cannot locate the borrowers).

Suppose you co-signed a car loan note for your brother-in-law. It costs you nothing to put your name on the note; the act will not appear in your check register. But when your brother-in-law takes off for Mexico and skips the payments, the bank will come after you to pay up. To ignore the fact that you are exposed for the amount of the note is to live in a fantasy land (where, most certainly, Uncle Sam would be a neighbor). Unfortunately, you, the taxpayer, are cosigning Uncle Sam's notes. If he ends up holding the bag, as so often happens, he simply sends you the bill, either through taxes, increased national debt, or by cheapening your savings and assets through depreciation of the currency.

The $630 billion of federal loan guarantees in force in 1990 does not count payment guarantees like Social Security, bank deposits insured by federal agencies, or various other purely insurance programs. That's the total for federally guaranteed loans—and nowhere in the unified budget does one find that enormous contingent liability. It is discussed in the budget document, but the enormous number appears nowhere in the actual budget.

That's not all. Our government also has something called "government sponsored enterprises" (GSEs). This category includes federally chartered corporations which the government is perceived as standing behind, whether there is an explicit obligation or not. The important GSEs are: the Farm Credit System and its two new auxiliary organizations, the Federal Home Loan Mortgage Corporation, the Federal National Mortgage Association, the Student Loan Marketing Association, and the Federal Asset Disposition Association. These and a few other GSEs now have outstanding borrowings of some $855 billion. The financial transactions of GSEs are shown in neither the unified budget nor the credit budget. Nonetheless, if a GSE falls on hard times, Uncle Sam will bail it out—and Congress will send you the bill.

## BUYING THE FARM

The classic GSE bailout is that of the Farm Credit System, which began in 1985. The system itself dates to 1916, and was designed to channel capital from financial centers like Chicago into rural areas where small country banks were unable to meet farmers' need for credit. (In 1916, remember, they didn't have our modern banking systems.)

Under the system, farmers would create and become stockholders of local Land Bank associations. When a farmer needed a loan, the association would provide it from funds advanced by one of twelve regional federal Land Banks. Farmers bought stock in the local association equal to five percent of the amount of their loan, and the local bought stock in the regional Land Bank in the same percentage. Eventually, farmer-borrowers retired the initial federal stock subscription to the Land Banks and became the owners of the entire system. So far so good; in fact it was a pretty soundly conceived and clever system, which took pride in being not a "government program," but "farmer owned."

By the early 1980s, however, farms across the country were folding by the hundreds. The rapid rise in farmland values through the 1970s, and the government's emphasis on big farms, export markets and efficiency, caused many farmers to expand beyond the bounds of prudence. They took on enormous debt loads, pledging their high-value farmland as collateral. When the farm land price bubble burst and farm prices collapsed, farmers defaulted and their local Land Bank associations went into bankruptcy. Nobody could

49

pay up the line, so ten of the twelve federal Land Banks came perilously close to bankruptcy. As one might suspect, the system's bookkeeping recognized farmland asset values well above what their true market value had become.

In September 1985 Congress cooked up its first bailout plan: basically "strict financial controls, but no cash." With the new accounting in place, the system reported to Washington that it was $4.2 billion in the hole. The administration did not want to allocate billions of dollars to cover this shortfall, so the system replied, "Very well, change the accounting system and the shortfall will magically go away."

But the Administration didn't want to relax the accounting rules either, having boasted about their effectiveness just months before. So the Farm Credit System blithely informed the president and Congress that unless some cash was poured into the system immediately, it would use the new accounting system to show the world that it was broke—right before the 1986 elections. This gambit was described, by a participant in the negotiations, as "Let's try some phony baloney accounting, or we can cause chaos."

The Administration caved in. It produced no cash at that point, but agreed to a bizarre formula whereby the dishonest bookkeeping would be made public along with a lengthy, technical note explaining that the foregoing accounts were highly suspect. The net effect was to convert dead losses into book assets, then write them off every year for twenty years, instead of all at once, as sound accounting practice requires. This caused GAO Chief Charles Bowsher to send a rare, unsolicited letter to congressional leaders warning that this scam would "turn back the clock to the earlier era of undisciplined accounting practice and loose credit analysis."

Despite this accounting gimmickry, investors weren't fooled, and in 1987 the system came back for the big handout. In January 1988 Congress gave birth to a new Farm Credit System Financial Assistance Corporation (FAC). As of June 1990 it had sold $1.172 billion of an authorized $3 billion of 15 year bonds fully guaranteed by the Treasury (read: the taxpayers). In addition to putting this taxpayer guarantee on the repayment of the bonds, Congress also provided that the Treasury (that's you, again) would pay the entire interest costs of the bonds for the first five years, and half of those costs for the next five years.

But that's not all! Congress also created the Farm Credit System Insurance Corporation. This new corporation would insure all the debt of the system other than that already guaranteed by the Treasury for FAC. By this time Congress was on a roll, so it created yet another GSE, the Federal Agricultural Mortgage Corporation. This entity would guarantee pools of farm mortgages originated by the federally guaranteed Land Banks, which in turn have been capitalized by the federally guaranteed FAC. If this seems confusing, take heart: not many congressmen understand it either.

**The result here is a massive, multi-billion-dollar web of guarantees and subsidies to bail out a privately owned credit system which, despite many years of success, had failed.** A major reason for that failure was an accounting system that led the system's managers to believe that things were fine when in fact debtors were losing their collateral value all over the place. (An encouraging note: in April 1991 the Treasury, GAO, and Congressional Budget Office agreed that increased government supervision of GSE operations, now involving more than a trillion dollars in outstanding securities, should be put in place quickly.)

## S&L: THE MOTHER OF ALL BAILOUTS

Our discussion now brings us to a truly world-class bailout, with numbers dwarfing the farm credit fiasco—the savings and loan bailout. **The S&L bailout ranks with the Interstate Highway System and World War II as one of the most massive taxpayer expenditures of all time.** But at least we got something useful out of World War II and the interstates.

The roots of the S&L crisis are complex, but the outline of the problem is easily understood. Until the end of the 1970s, S&Ls normally made housing mortgage loans, while commercial banks made commercial and industrial loans. The rate each type of institution could pay its depositors was fixed by Regulation Q of the Federal Reserve Board. Individual deposits for S&Ls were insured by the Federal Savings and Loan Insurance Corporation (FSLIC), and for banks by the Federal Deposit Insurance Corporation (FDIC). Insurance premiums for FSLIC were assessed on all S&Ls at a flat rate ($^{1}/_{12}$ of one percent of deposits) bearing no relation to the riskiness of the loan portfolio. Business practices of S&Ls were regulated by the Federal Home Loan Bank Board (FHLBB). Since S&Ls generally loaned to residential housing projects, which had been relatively stable and profitable investments since World War II, really tight regulatory supervision was not required, unless there was a suspicion of fraud.

By 1980, however, rampaging inflation had put S&Ls in an awful bind. Much of their asset portfolios consisted of old mortgages made when interest rates were five, six or seven percent. On the deposit side, Regulation Q limited the interest rate the S&Ls could pay to their depositors. With inflation at 12% and interest rates topping 20%, a 6.25% interest rate on a savings account did not look very attractive to depositors. In fact, inflation was actually robbing those who had invested at such a low rate. So depositors took their money out of S&Ls and put it into the new money market funds, which invested in short-term commercial paper bearing two or more times the rate of interest. The result was a cash hemorrhage; S&Ls couldn't bring in new deposits to make up for the money that was leaving.

This was obviously a recipe for industry insolvency, and in January 1981 some 1,715 S&Ls were technically broke. To cope with this calamity, Congress passed two major acts, in 1980 and 1982, directing the FSLIC and FHLBB to deregulate the lending industry. These new acts took the interest ceilings off deposited funds. They authorized S&Ls to invest in almost anything, largely eliminating the distinction in lending powers between S&Ls and commercial banks. The 1980 act also increased the deposit insurance from $40,000 to $100,000 per account—an action taken by the House-Senate conference committee with prior approval of neither House. (The Senate had approved an increase only to $50,000.) Somehow this radical increase swept through Congress with no one uttering a peep about it—or making a point of order which, unless overridden, would have killed the bill altogether. As a result of this new freedom, adventurous (that is, desperate) S&Ls went scrambling to attract deposits back from the money market funds. To get them back they had to offer very high interest rates. To earn enough from their assets to cover that interest, S&L managers sought out riskier and riskier investments. Many of those investments failed. So did many of the S&Ls. And the FSLIC, which insured the depositors, got stuck with the tab.

Of course, FSLIC had nowhere near enough reserves to meet the massive demand. So the FHLBB, which controlled the system, had to find ways to keep insolvent S&Ls from capsizing, and their customers from getting their deposits back from FSLIC. The result was "zombie thrifts," an apt term coined by Prof. Edward J. Kane of Ohio State University. In his book *The S&L Insurance Mess*, Kane writes, "The economic life they enjoy is an unnatural life-in-death existence in that, if they had not been insured, the firms' creditors would have taken control from stockholders once it became clear that their enterprises' net worth was exhausted. In effect a zombie has transcended its natural death from accumulated losses by the black magic of federal guarantees."

Here's how the accounting fudging made the zombie thrift problem worse. Suppose the zombie shows serious anticipated losses on many of its loans, and is heading for bankruptcy. But FSLIC and the FHLBB do not want that; it is far better for them that the wounded thrift struggle along for a few more years. Maybe something lucky will happen to bring it back to life; at worst, some of the regulators will have found other jobs or retired, leaving their successors to deal with the problem. Thus, in some documented cases, FHLBB regulators encouraged potential zombie thrifts to go out and make ever more risky loans, so the high interest received would enable the thrift to "grow its way out of trouble," at least in the short run. In the long run, of course, there is always the taxpayer to pay off the bills.

Meanwhile, irresponsible bidding for deposits to generate funds to put into riskier and riskier investments—by institutions which would long since have been auctioned off by a bankruptcy judge but for the federal deposit insurance protection and regulatory cowardice—drove the whole industry further out on the limb.

Notable in the creation of this crisis was the desperation-liberalized net-worth standard and the creative accounting used to convert financial fact into regulatory fiction. These bogus practices were authorized by a FSLIC facing bankruptcy itself. First, FSLIC, facing hundreds of collapsing institutions, made their traditional net worth requirement less stringent. Economists generally view a financial institution as undercapitalized when its ratio of net worth to assets falls below six percent. (For example, if a bank had assets of $100 million and liabilities of $94 million, its net worth would be

$6 million, and its net worth to assets ratio would be 6%.) Until 1978 the S&L industry standard was five percent; in 1980 FSLIC decided four percent was enough; two years later FSLIC made three percent acceptable. By 1984, even using generous accounting standards, 877 S&Ls, holding 31% of the insured institutions' assets, had fallen below the three percent level. If the requirement had been left at five percent and honest Generally Accepted Accounting Principles (GAAP) used, 2,090 S&Ls, with 79% of the assets, would have been substandard and subject to regulatory action.

Then there were FSLIC's Regulatory Accounting Practices (RAPs), the very name of which forbodes more government dishonesty. These pseudo-standards, described as "deceptively asymmetric" by economist Melanie Tammen of the Cato Institute, inflated the value of an institution's "goodwill" far beyond what any CPA would allow. ('Goodwill' is an intangible asset which attempts to reflect the value of customer support and confidence in an established institution. New enterprises do not have any of it.)

RAP also permitted S&Ls to book expected gains, however unrealistic, immediately, while allowing them to defer recognizing known losses. Columnist Warren Brookes has pointed out that when financier Charles Keating's Lincoln Savings and Loan Institution was finally taken over by the FSLIC in April 1989, it still had capital that exceeded the supposedly tough new capital standards enacted by Congress that August. Unfortunately, that "capital" was not reduced by Lincoln's undeclared loan losses, which, Brookes wrote, were more than enough to "chew up all that capital and then some." A tough capital standard is only as good as the quality of the capital it measures.

Another authorized accounting scam was to book as current income the full amount of fees paid at the origination of a loan, without allowing for the present value of the future costs of servicing the loan. To put it in laymen's terms, it's as if you rented someone an apartment, got the annual rental payment on day one, but made no allowance for paying your mortgage costs or property taxes on the building. Temporarily, you feel like you're rich, but you may well be insolvent by rigorous GAAP standards. Many S&Ls were.

Then there was a peculiar federal override of state S&L regulations, such as those in Texas. According to *U.S. News & World Report*, the Garn–St. Germain Act of 1982 allowed S&Ls to lend

100% of the appraised value of an asset—even if the actual purchase price was smaller. They say Texans think big, and this was no exception. Friendly Texas appraisers developed the habit of appraising at $15 million properties bought for $10 million, and the developers borrowed 100% of the higher figure. Indeed, fast-money artists bought up S&Ls and used them in this way to generate lots of loose change, knowing that when the institutions failed, as they certainly would, Uncle Sucker would bail out the depositors up to $100,000 per account.

Worst of all, the Garn–St. Germain Act gave S&Ls with insufficient net worth an ingenious method for looking good again. It allowed them to issue something called "net worth certificates," equal in value to Monopoly money, which, with a straight face, the S&Ls then turned over to FSLIC in exchange for FSLIC notes. "These notes," wrote Tammen, "are nothing more than unfunded promises of the insurance funds, put on paper to make believe that they would plug holes at decapitalized thrifts and banks."

**Unfunded promises masquerading as real value: there is no more certain indicator of accounting fraud. That Congress would deliberately authorize such a travesty is little less than a national disgrace. As Comptroller General Charles Bowsher said, "This is a huge scandal, and to a large extent it was allowed to grow because of the way this town does business."**

Despite all these ingenious—and dishonest—gimmicks, the financial status of the thrift industry slid downhill rapidly. Zombie thrifts multiplied like blobs from outer space in a seedy science fiction movie. When in 1987 the Reagan Administration bit the bullet and asked Congress for $15 billion to close down the worst of the zombies—a sum which might have been enough to do at least half of the job at the time—Congress almost shouted "No." (I shouted "yes," but was badly outvoted.) Why did Congress shout "No"? Because zombie thrifts were frantically lobbying key members of Congress (like former Speaker Jim Wright) *not* to vote the money that would make it possible for FSLIC to give them a decent burial. There was still looting to be done!

The S&L cycle of catastrophe is now clear: government price controls on interest; government insurance of $100,000 deposits; flat-rate deposit insurance premiums, regardless of the soundness of the institution; double-digit inflation; disintermediation—a flight of S&L deposits to higher yielding assets; capital hemorrhage; insolvency; asset deregulation; frantic financial wheeling and dealing; government-authorized bogus accounting; desperate efforts to buy influence in Congress; institutional collapse; and an astronomical bill sent to the taxpayers.

## PAYING THE S&L CLEANING BILL

Now that you know how the S&L crisis came about, let's look at the "solution," which is even more creative than the Farm Credit System bailout on which it was based. First, Congress creates a new GSE called the Resolution Trust Corporation. It borrows $50 billion from the viable parts of the S&L industry. These funds are turned over to FSLIC to cover the depositors' losses from zombie thrifts. Since these bonds are sold to the private sector, they are called "off budget." The Treasury, however, pays the interest on the bonds, on budget. And here is the really cute part: the payments from the Resolution Trust to FSLIC are deemed to be government revenue, which reduces the deficit, thus helping Congress meet the Gramm-Rudman-Hollings deficit reduction targets!

How big a price tag? In early 1989 the Administration was using the figure of $73 billion. By May 23, 1989, Treasury Secretary Nicholas Brady was telling Congress that twice as many zombie thrifts might not survive as previously estimated, and that costs would run anywhere from $89 billion to $132 billion. Meanwhile, the General Accounting Office was using a number of $155 billion. Then, on July 30, FDIC Chairman L. William Seidman upped the estimate of $175 billion to $200 billion. All of these estimates were in 1990 dollars. By June 1991 GAO offered a new estimate of $150 billion through 1992 alone, with more to come in following years.

The actual costs over thirty or forty years will, of course, be much higher. GAO estimated that the $155 billion cost of 1990 could amount to $500 billion over forty years: $155 billion in initial costs, $37 billion in administrative expenses, $133 billion in interest costs over 40 years, and a final $175 billion, if the optimistic projections of future interest rates prove to be unrealistic. That may not be a completely fair way to state the costs, but even the $132 billion is a staggering figure. Sen. Barbara Mikulski (D-MD) responded to Seidman's request for an indefinite appropriation to cover these costs by saying, "I'm concerned about writing a blank check." It's too bad she and the rest of the majority in Congress weren't so concerned a decade earlier, when this calamity was getting into high gear.

How much is a $132 billion bailout? With that much money, you could give 2,270,000 young people four-year scholarships to Harvard. You could give all 112 million American taxpayers a refund check of $1,170. More whimsically, the *Washington Times* calculated that you could pay the overdue fine at the Reston, Virginia public library for a book that was 36.1 million years overdue. But no matter how you add it up, the S&L bailout is the biggest taxpayer-absorbed bailout in history.

Why didn't the news media make this a page-one story sooner, when it was still manageable? Ellen Hume of Harvard's Shorenstein Barone Center on the Press, Politics, and Public Policy addressed that question in a perceptive column in the May 24, 1990 *New York Times*: "It was a 'numbers' story, not a 'people story.' It was all too complicated and boring to interest many mainstream journalists. Regulatory changes—such as accounting tricks and reduced capital requirements that helped paper over the first phase of the savings and loan crisis in the early 1980s—weren't big news." Television was particularly incompetent in dealing with this story. Hume quotes Michael Gartner, president of NBC News: "Television can't do facts." He might as well have added, "Americans aren't too good with numbers." Especially when the number is something like $132,000,000,000.

## EXPOSED ON ALL FRONTS

The S&L fiasco is bad enough, but it may not be the end of the calamities. The government—that is , the taxpayers—are exposed in many other ways as well. Commercial banks may suffer the same fate as many S&Ls if the economy and commercial real estate markets hit the skids. FDIC Chairman Seidman said in July 1990 that the deposit insurance fund, which insures $2.7 trillion of deposits, could see its assets shrink to $11 billion by year end. That would be the lowest reserve level in the 57-year history of the

FDIC, and half the level of reserves that most economists think prudent. Seidman had predicted earlier in the year that the fund would break even in 1990.

In August 1990 GAO projected bank failure losses of from $4.4 billion to $6.3 billion in 1990. A month later Comptroller General Bowsher told the Senate Finance Committee that current accounting methods masked the extent of the banks' problems. Even under GAAP accounting, banks can put off admitting losses until the last moment, preventing regulators from moving quickly to prevent catastrophic loss to the deposit insurance fund. "We are very much in need of a more realistic standard of accounting so that we're not just kidding ourselves about the extent of this problem," Bowsher said, "Not since its birth during the Great Depression has the federal system of deposit insurance for commercial banks faced such a period of danger and uncertainty as it does today."

At the same time economist R. Dan Brumbaugh of Stanford, a leading analyst of financial institutions, said that by strict accounting rules many banks—zombie banks, to parallel Kane's term for insolvent S&Ls—have already failed, but the FDIC lacks the funds to close them. Seidman vigorously disagrees with Brumbaugh's accounting requirements, but there is little doubt that, to use Seidman's term, the bank insurance fund is "severely stressed."

In December, Brumbaugh and colleagues Robert Litan and James Barth presented a lengthy report to the House Banking, Finance and Urban Affairs Committee. It concluded that the FDIC's Bank Insurance Fund was "in the same position as FSLIC was in the mid–1980s—without sufficient resources to pay for its expected case load of failed depositories." Their estimate of fund requirements for three years of a "mild recession" ranged from $19 billion to $43 billion.

In January 1991 the Congressional Budget Office weighed in with its projection: the fund would be $11 billion in the hole by the end of 1992—or as much as $40 billion if the recession proved to be longer and deeper than expected. Seidman called a hasty news conference to claim that a taxpayer bailout of the fund should not be necessary.

Only six weeks later, on February 28, Seidman unveiled a plan to borrow up to $30 billion over the next four years to keep the fund solvent. By April, Bowsher was reporting that the GAO audit of the fund showed assets of only $4 billion to $5 billion, well below the

$8.4 billion claimed by FDIC. The fund, Bowsher said, was "nearly insolvent," and the banks themselves in far weaker condition than previously calculated. While FDIC disputed GAO's audit figures, there was no disagreement that the fund would need either substantial premium increases, large new borrowings or taxpayer infusions to be able to cover the expected bank failure losses.

On June 10 Seidman raised his estimate again, from the previous $14.9 billion to $23.1 billion over the next eighteen months. At the same time Bowsher reported to the Senate Finance Committee that the Resolution Trust Corporation was in such disarray that it could not be audited by the GAO and that the ultimate cost of the rescue thus could not be calculated.

As if these colossal problems are not enough, there is the government pension plan insurance, run by the Pension Benefit Guaranty Corporation (PBGC). The PBGC steps in as pension trustee when a private pension plan is discontinued with insufficient funds for the promised benefits, and covers the shortfall with public funds. The most common case for PBGC action is a corporate bankruptcy. So far the PBGC is strong, supervising private pension trusts with over $1 trillion in assets, against some $800 billion in liabilities. Underfunding of pension plans is diminishing, and PBGC won a major Supreme Court case in 1990, which allowed it to order bankrupt corporations to reinstate terminated pension programs rather than unload their costs on the taxpayers.

Still, the PBGC fund is $1 billion in the red, and business failures of certain shaky corporations could drive the shortfall to $8 billion. This would require a premium increase that would encourage some employers to simply cancel their retirement plans, leaving their workers to fend for themselves after retirement.

Another troubling issue is what accountants call the "limited scope audit" of private pension plans under ERISA, the act which created the PBGC. ERISA authorizes auditors to accept the values of assets stated by banks and other administering institutions without further question. Given the manipulation of asset values so prevalent in the S&L scandal, how would anyone know whether the assets are really worth their assigned values? Accountants do not know, and so they add a disclaimer to their ERISA audit reports. Because of the disclaimer, says the Inspector General of the Labor Department, the audit reports are of "very little use." The American

Institute of CPAs has steadfastly complained about this problem. If it is not corrected, says the Inspector General, the audit requirement should be eliminated: "With almost half the plans producing disclaimers of opinion, money is being wasted on audits which provide no assurances or protections to participants." It would be far better to subject the guaranteed pension investments to thorough audits.

Nor do these exposures mark the end of it. There are also guaranteed student loans. In 1990 over $12 billion in new loans were guaranteed by the Department of Education—and loan defaults were estimated to reach $2 billion the same year. Despite the substantial subsidy, many loans go into default when students either can't or won't keep on making the payments.

## WASHINGTON, YOU'RE NO NEW YORK CITY

New York proved the point: dishonest accounting and financial management systems lead to big problems. Congress and the State of New York fixed the Big Apple's problems by insisting on the use of the rigorous GAAP standards. But Congress has been far less willing to impose the same tough standards on its own spending, lending and guaranteeing, and on its own flock of GSEs. And so, when calamity overtook the Farm Credit System and the thrift industry, a large part of the federal government's response was to concoct accounting devices—either to make it appear there was no problem or, failing that, give the impression that the problem was solved.

It should be clear by now that we as a nation cannot tolerate this kind of dangerous deception in our public accounting. The crises described in this chapter alone are enough to boggle the taxpayers's mind, as well as clean out his wallet. But, alas, there is more. There is the whole matter of federal retirement and pension systems, starting with the granddaddy of them all, Social Security.

# Chapter Five

---

# CONGRESSIONAL CHILD ABUSE: SEND THE KIDS THE BILL

---

FAR BE IT for me to criticize a poor Italian-American who, like many thousands of my father's countrymen, showed some entrepreneurial flair in his new country. Unfortunately, Charles Ponzi tried to do it dishonestly.

In Boston, back in 1920, he hit upon an idea: take in money from friends and promise to double it in a short period of time. For the idea to work honestly, he would have to ensure that the deposits more than doubled quickly, so he could make the promised payments and pocket some loose change for his trouble. Ponzi apparently thought he could do this by an investment scheme that didn't work. Rather than confessing failure, Ponzi fulfilled his promises to his first investors by using the payments from later investors. Money poured in, and as long as deposits outstripped payments by more than two to one, Ponzi was a going concern. Unfortunately, there weren't enough suckers in Boston for this deal to last. Ponzi went bust, and to jail. But he had achieved immortality: to this day, the term "Ponzi scheme" describes a get-rich-quick system based on making promises and taking in money faster than your customers discover that you can't keep the promises.

This background is useful when one examines the mythology of America's most important social program, Social Security—more precisely, the Old Age and Survivors Insurance program (OASI). (There are many other programs under the Social Security Act, such as Aid to Families with Dependent Children, Supplemental Security Income, and Medicare.) More than any other important federal program, Social Security has been deliberately misrepresented to many trusting people for many years. This is especially deplorable because Social Security has become absolutely vital to the retirement security of millions of Americans. **If there is any paramount duty of a member of Congress, beyond supporting the Constitution itself, it must be to protect Americans' legitimate expectations for the retirement security promised by the Social Security system. Any congressman not mindful of this obligation should expect—deservedly—to be promptly retired from public office.**

The OASI program began in 1935, when President Roosevelt and Congress enacted the first Social Security Act. The original program had two main goals: to provide a supplementary retirement income for the elderly, and to induce older workers to leave the labor force. This second goal may seem strange today, but in 1935 one plausible goal of public policy was to reduce massive unemployment by shrinking the number of workers seeking jobs.

The drafters of the original act sought to create a mandatory, government-run insurance company. Much was made of the idea that Social Security was a true insurance program, not a degrading welfare program. The House Subcommittee on Finance, in its report published in the *Congressional Record* of June 12, 1935, stated: "We can't ask support of a plan not at least as good as any American could buy from a private insurance company. The very least a citizen should expect is to get his money back upon retirement." If the new plan sought only that goal, one might wonder why it did not merely mandate that all workers provide retirement insurance for themselves. The answer is because such a mandate would not induce older workers to retire; they wouldn't have had time to accumulate a sufficient nest egg to do so.

The act required both employers and employees to pay one percent of the first $3,000 of annual earnings into a "trust fund." Upon retirement, the retiree would get the accumulated amount of the combined payments, plus interest. The rates would increase to three percent on employees and employers by 1949, after which the system would be financially sound at least until 1980. Everyone who paid the "contributions" was explicitly assured of getting at least that amount back, even if he or she were not eligible for the projected benefit stream.

Unfortunately, even for workers paying the maximum tax (then and now called a "contribution") of $30 a year, matched by the employer to $60, immediate retirement benefits were infinitesimal. One could be in the system for five years and retire with a Social Security annuity of two dollars a month. Clearly this was not going to help anyone soon, although young workers could expect to have a respectable retirement benefit after forty years of contributions. Thus the 74th Congress was faced with the specter of making general revenue welfare payments on behalf of hundreds of thousands of retirees who had paid very little into what was billed as an insurance system.

At the same time, the reserve fund was growing rapidly. Millions of workers and employers were paying in, and only a few were drawing out. With a growing trust fund balance, a need to entice workers to retire, and a fear of incurring large welfare payments for senior citizens, the solution was obvious: increase the benefits beyond what had been earned, and pay them out of the burgeoning reserves. Actuaries and accountants of that day quite correctly pointed out that at some fairly predictable future time, there would not be enough in the trust fund to pay benefits. But the politicians reasoned, as they often will, that such a scenario would be somebody else's problem later on.

In the original bill, the payroll tax and the benefit program had been kept carefully separate because of doubt about whether the Constitution allowed Congress to tax some people to benefit others. This sounds comical today, but in 1935 it was a live question. The Agricultural Adjustment Act of 1935 was in fact struck down by the Supreme Court in 1936 on the grounds that the tax it levied was linked to a regulatory scheme that went beyond the powers of the federal government.

Because of these constitutional concerns, any link between "contributions" (premiums) and benefits was deliberately disavowed in the passage, from political rhetoric to statute. When the constitutionality was tested in *Helvering v. Davis* (1937), the government's lawyers argued successfully that OASI was not insurance at all, but welfare. They convinced the Supreme Court that the "contributions" (taxes) were not tied to any particular benefit program. Harvard University Prof. Herman Leonard has observed that "the designers of the system clearly intended that its payroll taxes be so synonymous in the minds of the contributors with old age benefits that no Congress could ever divert them to any other purpose. (But) the constitutionality of the act was upheld on the grounds that, as written, it was not a mandatory public insurance program—which, of course, was exactly what it was and what it absolutely had to be to survive politically."

The case of *Fleming v. Nestor* in 1960 completed the government's legal repudiation of the insurance idea, although politically the idea is promoted as earnestly as ever. In that case the Court held that Congress had the right to cut off promised "insurance" benefits to a suspected Communist who had fled the country. Justice Hugo Black, who had been a senator when OASI was enacted, dissented sharply, observing that the majority had declared that Congress was giving the citizen "something for nothing, and it can stop doing so when it pleases. I cannot believe that any private insurance company in America would be permitted to repudiate its matured contracts with its policyholders who have regularly paid all the premiums in reliance upon the good faith of the company." He was quite right, of course: What had been sold to the nation in 1935 as an insurance program had by 1960 become a program, the benefits of which could be changed, taxed away or withdrawn by a Congress possessing any remotely believable rationale.

But even after repeatedly denying in court that the OASI program was a public insurance system, the government relentlessly promoted that politically popular, but deceptive, idea. An early information booklet advised workers that their payroll deductions were "strictly accounted for and kept separate from the general funds of the U.S. Treasury," which was clearly false. As late as 1973, Wilbur J. Cohen, a key draftsman of the original act and secretary of Health, Education and Welfare under President Johnson, was declaring with a straight face that the OASI system was "government insurance" which provided a "legal right to benefits backed by a guarantee from the federal government and legal recourse to the courts for payment."

The "trust fund," of course, had long since evaporated, its monies having been used to pay current beneficiaries in amounts far greater than the accumulated value of their payments and those of their employers. As David Stockman later put it, "The politicians had sweetened nearly everybody's earned pension with extra dollars for dependents, low earnings, and numerous other concepts of 'need' that had nothing to do with what a worker had put into the fund. . . . Unearned benefits severed the existing actuarial linkage between what you put into the fund and what you got out of it. Once the linkage was gone, the politicians were off to the races, adding promise after promise of unearned benefits to those who retired by mortgaging the incomes of workers not yet born. By 1980 Social Security had become a giant Ponzi scheme."

The institution of the "pay-as-you-go" principle put an end to the possibility of an actuarially sound trust fund accumulation, although Social Security publications continued to tout the idea of a "trust fund," to reassure workers that their retirement was securely provided for. The retention of the insurance rhetoric was, as economist Barbara Wootton pointed out, "an increasing element of fiction." (And that was in 1955!)

For many, the disappearance of any actuarially sound trust fund was a relief. In 1935 Treasury Secretary Henry Morgenthau, who was hooked on the insurance idea, had favored the accumulation of large reserves to meet liabilities of workers retiring in the 1960s and 1970s. But others, including many conservatives, were convinced that the investment of huge Social Security reserves in private sector securities would make the government a silent partner in much of the private economy.

By 1981, just four years after Congress's much-touted "fix" of the system (via higher tax rates), the OASI "trust fund" took in at the beginning of a month barely enough to cover checks issued at the end of a month. In 1982 the OASI fund borrowed funds for the first time ever, from the only slightly more solvent health insurance (Medicare) fund. The following year a bipartisan National Commission on Social Security Reform produced an agreement, soon ratified by Congress, which accelerated planned increases in social security tax rates and coverage limits between 1984 and 1990. Coupled with five years of a very strong economy, the taxes rolled in, and by 1989 the "trust fund" had developed a surplus of $56 billion. Unless the tax rates are changed, the fund is projected to grow to $103 billion by 1993, about enough to pay 16 months' benefits. By 2015 the reserves will peak at five years' worth of benefits. By 2048 the OASI fund will be dead broke again, unless benefits are curtailed or new revenues are raised somewhere along the way.

The implications of a hand-to-mouth Social Security system are fairly obvious: any unexpected economic reverse will throw the system into bankruptcy and jeopardize the vital interests of millions of older Americans. The financial management implications of a large Social Security trust fund are less obvious. What happens when income rises faster than outgo? The Treasury spends the payroll tax receipts as fast as it can get its hands on them. In their place—in the so-called "fund"—it leaves an IOU. This piece of paper is the Treasury's promise to scrounge up the required amount of cash on the due date of the IOUs. As OMB Director Richard Darman put it in 1989, **"The related trust funds that pretend to hold 'surpluses' for future beneficiaries in fact hold hundreds of billions of dollars in unfunded IOUs. These are a little surprise for the workers of tomorrow left by the consumers of today."**

By law, the "trust fund" can only be invested in this Treasury paper. Where will it get the cash to redeem the IOUs? Barring an unlikely federal surplus, probably from selling more Treasury bonds. So, instead of accumulating real assets, the "trust fund" accumulates only more special government IOUs.

To make matters worse, as Senator William Proxmire pointed out as far back as 1981, the "investments" bought by the Secretary of the Treasury are special Treasury bonds issued only to the trust funds. At a time when federal security mutual funds were getting over 13% return, the Social Security trust fund was getting only an 8% return. This suggests that the Secretary of the Treasury was more interested in holding down the cost of his borrowings than in increasing the investment yield for Social Security beneficiaries of today and tomorrow. If a private trust company did this it almost certainly would face lawsuits from depositors and disciplinary action from the banking authorities. (The technical argument that the interest rate paid on illusory assets is also largely hypothetical does not in my view diminish the gravity of the offense.)

Prof. Leonard says, quite correctly, that "the current system produces a strong temptation to spend the money raised for Social Security twice. The accumulated reserves can be spent in practice without touching them in principle or on paper. . . . Spending the money twice will ultimately require raising it twice. When Social Security beneficiaries present their claims, there will be no real choice but to pay them. Taxpayers who first put up the money to fund Social Security benefits through the reserves, and then watched as that money was siphoned off to permit more current government spending, would then be forced either to abrogate the political commitments of the Social Security system . . . or reluctantly to fund Social Security again."

The cash pilfered from the fund is spent on the things the federal government buys every day—aircraft carriers, national parks, bureaucrats' salaries, foreign aid, food stamps, etc. The Social Security surplus reduces the deficit, but eventually someone will have to pay taxes to redeem the IOUs the Treasury left when it grabbed the cash. Who will be saddled with that bill? Your kids and grandkids. That's why Social Security has become the congressional equivalent of child abuse.

This is all bad enough, but there is more. In 1985 Congress took OASI out of the so-called unified budget, where it had been since 1969. Until 1991 OASI balances were still used in calculating compliance with the Gramm-Rudman-Hollings (GRH) deficit-reduction targets. Using present Congressional Budget Office (CBO) estimates, in 1993 OASI surpluses will cancel or mask $103 billion of what CBO projects to be a deficit from all other activities of $233 billion. The net "unified budget deficit," instead of being $233 billion, will be only (!) $130 billion. In other words, according to the CBO the non-Social Security deficit will grow by $22 billion from 1989 to 1993, but, thanks to the growth of the Social Security surplus, the total net deficit will go down. Without these mushrooming Social Security surpluses, the GRH goals would have become hopelessly unreachable.

The obvious "solution" to this sort of whitewash was to remove Social Security from the GRH calculation. Both liberals and conservatives in Congress favored doing this, but for completely different reasons. The liberals believed that it would reveal a "true" deficit far too large to be eliminated by GRH spending restraints, demanding new taxes on "the rich and the big corporations," which even the conservatives would be forced to support. The conservatives, on the other hand, thought the trust fund surplus reduced the pressure on Congress to cut back on spending. Unfortunately, both were right. They joined in the 1990 Budget Enforcement Act to remove Social Security balances from the deficit calculation which, if the deficit is "too large," triggers automatic spending reductions. The vote in the House was an astonishing 413–15.

But that is a political debate, not a financial management one. The real question is whether to let the fund build a surplus or not, and if so, what to do with the money. If funds are allowed to build up, we could continue as at present, replacing the cash with IOUs and passing the bills on to future generations. That is obviously a disgraceful idea—which is, of course, no reason why Congress won't do it. Alternatively, we could invest the surplus in "real" assets instead of mere Treasury IOUs.

Wall Street has had a long love-hate relationship with this latter idea. It would promise a colossal stock and bond market boom by bringing hundreds of billions of payroll tax dollars into the financial markets. On the other hand, it would raise the specter of government control of corporations that alarmed conservatives in the Thirties. It would also increase Treasury's massive interest costs generally.

Another option would be to invest only in government-approved, public-sector securities, rather than in private-sector issues. This eliminates the specter of government control of the private economy, but raises a host of new problems. As economist Paul Craig Roberts has pointed out, there would be great pressure for the trust fund managers to "invest" the funds in state and local "infrastructure" bonds (quite possibly just before elections), debt issued by bankrupt Third World countries and off-loaded on the fund by the large international banks, and securities issued to bail out bankrupt savings and loans and farm credit banks, etc. As Roberts concludes, "the 'trust fund' will show holdings of 'guaranteed' securities, and all of the accounting will be legal. **Nevertheless, a scam will have been perpetrated, and the 'trust fund' will consist of nothing but the government's ability to raise taxes to redeem its IOUs."**

68

What if the funds were used to purchase and retire federal debt in the market? That would merely perpetuate the present deficit spending, for new debt would probably be issued as fast as old debt would be bought back. Even if new debt were not issued, the idea of using a payroll tax to retire federal debt is terribly ill-conceived. Imagine taxes being taken out of working people's paychecks to produce capital gains for those fortunate enough to own government bonds. Working people, quite rightly, would never stand for it.

This depressing analysis leads to an examination of whether to restrain the buildup to a ceiling of, say, 18 months' worth of fund disbursements. There are two ways to do this. One is just to increase the benefits at once; that would, of course, make a lot of beneficiaries very happy, but since politics would prevent benefits from ever being reduced again, an increase would merely ratchet the system further out of control as future beneficiaries appeared to claim the higher payments. The remaining solution is to stop the accumulation, not by increasing benefits that will saddle future generations, but by reducing the payroll tax burden on the present working generation. That was the solution advocated on the last day of 1989 by Sen. Daniel Patrick Moynihan, chairman of the Senate Subcommittee on Social Security. His idea to "give it back" did not come to a vote until April 24, 1991, when it was tabled 60–38 under strong Bush Administration pressure.

What would happen if the payroll tax rates were cut to eliminate the surplus, say to 5.2% (10.4% total) on the first $69,300 of earnings (the eventual Moynihan proposal)? Obviously, all the problems of the mushrooming trust fund would be eliminated. Lowering the "tax on labor" would make U.S. labor more competitive in world markets. Or, if the tax rate cut were linked to some form of individual savings account, as President Bush has recommended, the proceeds of the cut could be channeled from those millions of accounts into productive investments in the private economy—without running the risk of private sector control by government investment funds. This latter combination of ideas forms the core of proposals over the years from Nobel-prize-winning economist James Buchanan, policy analysts Charles D. Hobbs, Stephen Powlesland, and Peter Ferrara, and former Delaware Gov. Pete duPont. A similar system was put in place in Chile over a decade ago, and it has been very well accepted. Congressman John Porter (R-IL) has been the most articulate advocate for such a plan in Washington, which he calls the Individual Social Security Retirement Account. It is an idea well worth exploring.

If such a system were put into place here, individuals could make a genuine contribution to their own fully funded retirement security plan, instead of having their paychecks skimmed to feed Washington's apparently insatiable spending habit. The problems of the large fund, the insurance-government program debate, and fictitious government accounting would be solved. **Provisions to redeem promises already made to older workers and present retirees would require many billions of dollars in resources, but those moral commitments to retirement security are utterly inviolable and could not be evaded in any case. In fact, the more one thinks about it, the more this looks like the smartest way to go. Honest accounting and genuine investment in our economy is a combination one rarely finds in federal government programs.**

# Chapter Six

# A HOUSE OF ILL REPUTE: DO AS I SAY, NOT AS I DO

THERE WERE TEN of us, Republican members of Congress, gathered on the grassy knoll across from the House wing of the Capitol on that summer day in 1987. We were there to unveil a joint product, a collection of studies on the workings of the House of Representatives.

Indignant at how the majority party was mismanaging the House, we had worked long and hard to condense our views into ten hard-hitting chapters. In them we dwelt on the majority's seemingly unrestrained penchant for spending money we didn't have. We inveighed against lavish spending on creature comforts for congressmen, bloated staff budgets, falsified transcripts, parliamentary tyranny, ethical failures—a catalog of disgrace.

Naturally all ten of us wanted a turn before the camera. Even though we were all friends and collaborators, each of us, being politicians, was thinking, "The electronic media will snip out of this presentation only the piece best suited to 30 seconds of evening news. How can I be sure that it will feature *me*?" This was a particularly distressing problem for me, since I wasn't a national celebrity like Newt Gingrich, a charmer like Barbara Vucanovich or someone with the recognition of a Connie Mack (now a U.S. Senator from Florida).

So when my turn came, I said, "I don't mean to sound like Cecil B. DeMille here, but . . . ," then I turned with a grand sweep of the hand toward the Capitol dome: "Behold! A House of Ill Repute!"

Unfortunately, my theatrical efforts did not make the night's network news, but the phrase stuck. To reinforce it, the cover of our book featured a drawing of the Capitol dome, topped with a garish red light bulb in place of the goddess of Freedom.

I must confess that my glib title pained me a bit, as it did the others. True, there were plenty of facts to back up our harsh characterization, but we really wanted the Congress to regain its place in the public's mind as the nation's (and, perhaps, the world's) great and respected parliament. We deeply regretted that the House, the chamber which each of us had worked so hard to join, had become, in many ways, "a house of ill repute." The only way we knew to restore the House—and Congress as a whole—to respect was to face the situation squarely, lay out the case for reform, and hope that an aroused citizenry, and perhaps a shamed House leadership, would clean up the mess.

When you've lived in a house a long time, some day you awake to the fact it's getting ratty: the walls are dirty, the carpet worn; the furnace makes strange wheezing sounds; the windows don't quite shut and the furniture is scuffed and ragged. You remember all the maintenance over the years, and wonder how the place could have gotten so grimy without anyone noticing. When the first crack appeared on the leather armchair, you oiled it carefully to head off further damage—but now there are a hundred cracks in it. While you were thinking about other things, the place went to ruin.

**That's what has happened to Congress after decades of quiet deterioration, ethical carelessness, slipshod management, and growing tolerance of unfair and dishonest fiscal practices.**

Our indictment in 1987 covered ground familiar to anyone acquainted with the daily headlines and evening news at that time. Unfortunately, despite the forced resignations of Speaker Jim Wright and Majority Whip Tony Coelho in 1989, little has been done to redeem Congress from the accumulated grime and disrepair.

Look at Congress' continuing resolve to increase its own legislative empire. Georgia Congressman Newt Gingrich recalls the day in 1985 when 133 Democrats voted four times in a row to defeat Republican effort to curb the expansion of the House budget and benefits the House majority regularly showers upon itself. Newt calls these 133 individuals "the spendaholics," because they are irrevocably committed to expanding the House empire, a bastion of privilege and comfort.

The late and much-loved Congressman Silvio Conte was one of the deans of the House, a silver-haired Republican from the western reaches of Massachusetts, and ranking Republican on the House Appropriations Committee. In that 1985 debate he observed that in his first year in Congress in 1959 there were ten parking garage attendants in the House and Senate combined; twenty-six years later the number had blossomed to over one hundred, although there were still the same number of members. "What are they doing down there?" he asked. "Go and look. They are sitting around in groups of two, three, or four, just talking to each other and watching the cars go by."

He went on to point out that any legitimate security problems in the congressional garages ought to be handled by some of the 1,227 Capitol police (about seven policemen per acre of the Capitol grounds, including the Supreme Court and Library of Congress). Or, he went on, perhaps some of the 72 House and Senate "doorkeepers" could pitch in in an emergency. "We had 42 of these doorwatchers when I came to Congress and I can't for the life of me find any more doors to the floor or the gallery than we had then," said Conte.

Conte's amendment to reduce the number of parking lot attendants was shouted down to defeat. Every one of those attendants and doorkeepers "belonged" to some member of Congress, and none wanted to give any of them up.

Hank Brown of Colorado, now a senator, was one of the real taxpayers' champions in the House. He offered a very modest amendment to freeze the number of "operators" for the automatic elevators in the House office buildings. No luck. The spendaholics added 20% to the automatic elevator operator fund, presumably so that there would be enough spares around to step in if the burden of operating an automatic elevator became too severe for someone on duty. One Republican member started out to use the story of the automatic elevator operators in a stump speech, and discovered that his rural Georgia constituents simply didn't believe it was true.

Newt Gingrich incisively pointed out why the majority party won't agree to curb legislative spending: to rise in the ranks of the House Democratic caucus, you have to keep your colleagues happy, and you cannot do so by cutting out their parking lot attendants and automatic elevator operators. If you make a career out of curbing such practices, when your time comes to enter the leadership, you'll have no friends—just a roomful of colleagues itching to get even for the embarrassment and discomfort you have brought them over the years.

The General Accounting Office reported in February 1990 that on any given day the House Bank, a free financial service for members, was holding 30 checks on members' accounts for insufficient funds, and that on the 12 days sampled more than 90 members had written bad checks. In September 1991 a further GAO study reported that four thousand rubber checks had been cashed by the House Bank during a six month period. California Republican Bob Dornan, who put this latest GAO report in the news, calls these Congressional check-kiters "bozos." Columnist Christopher Mathews picked up on it to ask, "Is there a connection between this mammoth fiscal irregularity in the federal budget and the bozolike behavior at the House Bank? Of course there is. The same people (who) vote upstairs bank downstairs." Not all Congressmen are passing bad checks on their personal accounts, of course, but year after year Congress as a body is writing bad checks in the form of budget bills that exceed the account balance by hundreds of billions of dollars. I guess the check-bouncing scandal should not come as much of a surprise.

## LAWS NEED NOT APPLY

The concern that Congress might feather its own nest arose more than 200 years ago. In the Federalist Papers, published in 1788, James Madison tried to anticipate such a situation. He observed that those opposing the government plan set forth in the new Constitution objected that House members would be from that class of citizens "most likely to aim at an ambitious sacrifice of the many to the aggrandizement of the few."

Madison offered five reasons why this outcome would be unlikely, the fifth of which is the most interesting. Congress, he said, "can make no law which will not have its full operation on themselves and their friends, as well as on the great mass of society. This has always been deemed one of the strongest bonds by which human policy can connect the rulers and the people together." Madison declared that Congress would modestly refrain from feathering its own nest because of "the genius of the whole system; the nature of just and constitutional laws; and above all, the manly spirit which actuates the people of America—a spirit which nourishes freedom, and in return is nourished by it. **If this spirit shall ever be so far debased as to tolerate a law not obligatory on the legislature, as well as on the people, the people will be prepared to tolerate anything but liberty."**

**With all due respect to James Madison, that argument turned out to be bunk.**

Senator Charles Grassley (R-IA) has compiled a list of burdensome laws which most Americans have to struggle under, but from which Congress cleverly has exempted itself:

- The Social Security Act of 1935
- The National Labor Relations Act of 1935
- The Fair Labor Standards Act of 1938
- The Equal Pay Act of 1963
- The Civil Rights Act of 1964
- The Freedom of Information Act of 1966
- The Age Discrimination Act of 1967
- The Occupational Safety and Health Act of 1970
- The Equal Employment Opportunity Act of 1972
- The Higher Education Amendments of 1972, Title 9
- The Rehabilitation Act of 1973
- The Privacy Act of 1974
- The Age Discrimination Act Amendments of 1975
- The Ethics and Government Act of 1978
- The Civil Rights Restoration Act of 1988

Senator Grassley points out that the burdens imposed on ordinary Americans by these acts can be enormous:

If any business person runs afoul of the above mentioned laws, the full weight of Federal coercion will likely fall on them. That means, at

75

a minimum, Federal court litigation and harassment by Federal bureaucrats. Anyone sued under these statutes knows the feeling. Anyone harassed by a Federal bureaucrat knows the feeling. But the authors of these laws worry not. They are not covered. No government lawsuits against them; no bureaucratic harassment; no "private rights of action," either. Indeed, there is no remedy against Congress. This breeds contempt among the public. It says to the common man that Congress thinks it's above the law.

That contempt is measurable. In a survey conducted by the Louis Harris organization in 1986, only 34% of the respondents had a positive view of members of Congress, while 58% had a negative view. (Respondents viewed my profession of Certified Public Accountant as more positive than negative by a 57–21 margin—tied with doctors for the widest positive spread.) I daresay that the public's view of Congress in 1992 would be even less enthusiastic.

When the Senate debated the "Civil Rights Act of 1990" in July of that year, Grassley put his fairness concept to a vote, with interesting results. The Civil Rights Act, known to opponents as the "Kennedy-Hawkins Racial Quotas Bill," was drafted to reverse several recent Supreme Court decisions having to do with defense of employers against charges of racial discrimination in employment. Amidst inflated rhetoric about racism and nondiscrimination, Grassley proposed to make three of the foregoing laws cover employment discrimination by the Senate itself.

Perhaps shamed into submission, the Senate agreed. But when it came to giving aggrieved Senate employees the same rights as their private sector counterparts, the Senators balked. The Senate was willing to let its employees complain to the Senate Select Committee on Ethics. But to federal court? No way. The Grassley amendment, which would have allowed a plaintiff to appeal a Senate panel's decision to federal court, was rejected by a vote of 63–26. Said Grassley, the substitute measure approved "makes equal rights an illusion on Capitol Hill. It will ensure that Congress will never live under the same law that applies to the rest of America."

In the House, Congressman Bill Dannemeyer tried to offer a similar proposal to the popular Americans with Disabilities Act, described by its backers as an "emancipation proclamation" for the handicapped. Dannemeyer offered his amendment—to provide the act's remedies to House employees—in several committees as the bill moved toward floor action. It was rejected. He was denied permission to offer it as a floor amendment, so the House members would not get caught on a roll call.

As a fig leaf, the House grudgingly allowed its handicapped employees to appeal, not to a court, but to the House Office of Fair Employment Practices. And what happens in the unlikely event that this Office awards a monetary remedy to a staff member? The award would be paid, not from the expense account of the member guilty of the discrimination, but from the House contingency fund. The offending member would pay nothing out of his own pay and allowances; the taxpayer would get the tab for compensation, back pay and attorney's fees.


## FORTRESS OF INCUMBENCY

Does the public respond to such double-dealing by cleaning out Congress with a big, swift broom every two years? Unfortunately, no. More than 98% of House members seeking reelection win. They win despite their scofflaw antics, despite horrendous budget deficits, despite continuing ethical scandals, and despite engaging in gross budgetary and fiscal negligence and mismanagement.

They win reelection because of carefully engineered incumbent advantages: gerrymandered districts, the free-mail franking privilege, the excessive staff salaries (in 1990, $433,900 per House office), the Capitol radio and television studios, and the very generous expense accounts for phone, travel and office space. The *Washington Times* has totaled the representative's expenses: $941,569 per year. Unlike the executive agencies, which must secure the approval of the House Appropriations Committee when a proposed shift exceeds ten percent of a budget figure, House members can shift $50,000 back and forth, no questions asked.

The franking privilege is notably subject to abuse. In May 1990 the U.S. Postal Service projected that the House would exhaust the allotted $41 million for mailings four months before the end of the fiscal year. That was because the House set an all-time record of 130,000,000 pieces of mail in the first three months of that election year. What happens if the funds run dry? No problem: the House members just keep sending out the mail, producing a projected $38 million cost overrun. The Senate, to its credit, has tightened up on use of the frank. But when Senators Harry Reid (D-NV) and Don Nickles (R-OK) urged House Speaker Tom Foley to support similar reforms in the House, they were told by the Speaker that "this is one expenditure the public appears to approve of."

Even when they've stopped sending tons of such "useful" junk mail, members perpetuate their perks through another means: their congressional pensions. Take the case of former Rep. Dan Mica (D-FL). At age 45, he left the House in January 1989 after 19 years service. He served one more year as a consultant to his former Committee, the House Committee on Foreign Affairs, to get in the magic twenty years of eligibility. According to Matthew Cooper of the *Washington Monthly*, this final year qualified Mica for an annual pension of $36,054. If his life is of average length, Mica will pull down at least $2.5 million in pension payments. The National Taxpayers Union found that the pension of former Speaker Jim Wright, who resigned from the House in disgrace, will start at $83,070 a year and approach a total of $2 million over a normal life expectancy.


AMERICANS OUGHT TO be proud of their national legislature. They deserve to look upon the Capitol building and feel that it is a shrine of democracy, inhabited by men and women who have "the high honor and distinct privilege" of serving honorably and well.

It is time that the people demanded a thorough cleaning of what many citizens now see as a "house of ill repute"—an end to outrageous and costly perquisites, an end to ethical carelessness, an end to special exemptions from the laws the rest of us live by, an end to every cozy little deal which insulates our representatives from the standards and reality of the rest of America, and an end to what can only be described as legal election rigging to ensure that no one is ever defeated for reelection.

Members of Congress win reelection despite an insatiable lust for MORE MONEY—not more money in recognition of outstanding work, but more money for doing no more than continuing poor fiscal performance and chronic financial deception. Being so certain of reelection, they feel little pressure to clean house—and so they don't.

Isn't it time that we, the people, do?

# Chapter Seven

---

# HONEST ACCOUNTING, DISCIPLINED BUDGETING, CLEAR REPORTING

---

SOMETIMES YOU KNOW where you are and where you want to go—but you've got a defective map and a broken-down vehicle. That's the situation Congress is in when it comes to budgetary issues. In recent years, thoughtful politicians of both parties, skilled technicians in the General Accounting Office (GAO) and the accounting profession, financial experts in the executive branch—all have contributed useful thinking to straightening out the budgetary tangle. The outlines of reform are becoming well-known. What is still lacking is a strong will to get the job done.

As an accountant in private practice, I often found myself trying to straighten out clients who had good intentions but bad bookkeeping practices. After 22 years I found that the best approach is to make up a step-by-step list of what it takes to convert a poor set of books into a good set. This is no secret. Every good CPA does the same thing, making use of appropriate accounting principles and practices.

Admittedly, applying Generally Accepted Accounting Principles to the federal government is much more difficult and uncertain than applying them to even a large multinational, multi-industry private sector enterprise. The government would demand even greater attention to the process by which budgetary decisions are made and the kind of information the system provides to the decision makers, including the 535 members of Congress.

Nonetheless, I believe basic reforms can and should be made right now; refinements, enhancements, and the quest for perfection can come later on. What follows is a seven-step program for getting the federal government back on track.

## REFORM ONE: INSTALL ACCRUAL ACCOUNTING

As we discussed in Chapter Three, the federal government must abandon its antiquated mom-and-pop style cash accounting system in favor of more sophisticated accrual accounting, which reflects actual liabilities and future commitments. Since cash basis accounting ignores government obligations to spend money in the future, it gives a disastrously incomplete and inaccurate picture of where the government really stands. It also predictably allows legislators to favor today's voters at the expense of tomorrow's taxpayers.

I believe that the biggest single problem we face today in federal accounting is the huge amount of debt and contingent liability that is off the books. The press and public is rapidly catching onto this problem, as the savings and loan crisis blossoms into a taxpayer burden of $132 billion to $500 billion.

**Congress' motto seems to be "Out of sight, out of mind" whenever the question of accrual accounting is raised. Unfortunately, what is out of sight today—tomorrow's bills—will surely come back like Marley's ghost to haunt future Congresses and taxpayers alike. With rigorous accrual accounting we are forced to face the true financial facts now, instead of enduring sudden and ugly surprises later.**

We badly need capital budgeting and accounting that more accurately matches the cost of capital outlays (and inflated replacement value) with the useful life of the asset purchased. This is, in a sense, the flip side of the unrecorded liability; in effect, the "one year lifetime" asset. (Unfortunately, from a solvency standpoint, our unrecorded liabilities far exceed our unrecorded assets.)

It is obviously ridiculous to "expense" major capital items—write them off in only the first year when they may have a 30- or 40-year lifetime. Not only is this false accounting, but it results in a bias against capital investment. (If the budget has to take the full hit the first year, the chances of Congress approving the expenditure are reduced.) And, as a result, the executive branch develops a bias toward renting instead of buying or building, which clearly would be more economical over the useful life of the asset.

Moreover, we should adopt the GAO-recommended division of the budget into three major accounts: general, trust fund and enterprise. This division would flow naturally from adopting accrual accounting and capital budgeting, and would make budget documents far more understandable. All agency accounts should be strictly reviewed by outside auditors, and an easy-to-read overall financial statement of the federal government enclosed with the IRS package sent to taxpayers each January. (The House Republican Research Committee, co-chaired by Reps. Chris Cox (R-CA) and Sonny Callahan (R-AL), issued a pioneering version in 1990, covering fiscal 1990.)

## REFORM TWO: AGREE ON ECONOMIC PROJECTIONS

It is no easy matter predicting the GNP and rates of inflation, interest and unemployment a year in advance. And it should not be surprising that competing branches of the federal government—the president and the Congress—arrive at different economic projections. The projections are often skewed for political reasons, but even if they weren't, there still would be plenty for reasonable people to differ over.

Comptroller General Charles Bowsher has testified that "there has been a persistent pattern of overly optimistic budget assumptions and projections, and the trend may be continuing. For example, the House and Senate budget resolutions for fiscal 1989 contained an estimated deficit of about $134 billion. This figure was based on OMB's economic assumptions, considered very optimistic by many observers. The less optimistic Congressional Budget Office (CBO) economic assumptions, however, placed the baseline deficit in 1989 at $176 billion." (The actual fiscal 1989 deficit turned out to be $152 billion, giving a range for the estimates of −12% to +16%.)

In recent years, the executive branch has made progress toward arriving at a consensus on economic numbers. It is called the "troika" process, because it involves three players: the OMB Director, the Treasury Secretary, and the Chairman of the Council of Economic Advisers. Once the troika agrees on key economic variables, those variables are used throughout the president's budget. But the troika numbers differ from private market projections because they assume the adoption and implementation of the Administration's program, which Congress may or (more likely) may not do.

It is easier to recommend having a consensus economic forecast than actually hammer one out between Congress and the executive. Nonetheless, it should be possible to arrive at a formula—including weighted contributions from various public- and private-sector models based on their past track records, and realistic expectations of congressional action on the president's proposals—that would come much closer to reality than what is now being used. A government that generates economic numbers via the equivalent of Murray Weidenbaum's "visceral computer" is not a government whose numbers will be taken seriously.

## REFORM THREE: MOVE TO A BIENNIAL BUDGET

A two-year budget cycle would have many positive effects. Since some 60% of all congressional roll call votes now involve budget-related issues, the two-year cycle ought to spread the same number of votes (and hours of debate) over two years, leaving a lot of additional time for badly needed program oversight. Under a biennial budget, Congress would have to pass in the second year only those appropriations bills already agreed to in the first year. The appropriations process itself could also be switched to a two-year cycle.

The Defense Department already has switched to a two-year cycle because much of its expenditures (force levels) are stable and recurring, and much of the rest (procurement) requires multi-year planning. There also would be only half as many potential "running-out-of-money" crises with two-year budgeting.

In 1987 Congress and the president agreed to a two-year budget plan for fiscal years 1988 and 1989. This accord allowed Congress—for the first time since 1977—to pass all 13 appropriations bills without using continuing resolutions. In his fiscal 1990 and fiscal 1991 budget messages, President Bush proposed a permanent two-year cycle, noting, however, that it must be accompanied by strict discipline so that supplemental appropriations bills are not routinely used to change the deal halfway through. This proposal disappeared from his fiscal 1992 budget message, but should be revived.

## REFORM FOUR: ENHANCE PRESIDENTIAL RESCISSION AUTHORITY

Rescission authority is the power Congress gives the president to propose reductions in spending already voted. Since the 1974 Budget Reform Act, the president must propose rescissions to Congress, which need not act on them. They can just yawn, go about their business, and, after 45 days of congressional inaction, the rescissions fail. President Reagan won some significant rescission votes in the wake of his smashing 1980 election victory, but since then the great majority of proposed rescissions have disappeared without a trace on Capitol Hill. In fact, in President Reagan's last four years only 8 of 164 proposed rescissions were approved, totaling just $183 million out of $16 billion. That's about 1 percent of the total cuts requested.

Enhanced rescission authority puts the shoe on the other foot: the rescissions go into effect unless Congress acts to disapprove them within a specified time limit. Senators Dan Coats (R-IN) and John McCain (R-AZ) have led the fight for this important tool.

## REFORM FIVE: ENFORCE THE 1990 BUDGET ENFORCEMENT ACT

The new spending discipline mechanisms provided by this act have been described in Chapter 1. The House vote on the first day of the

1991 session, which transfered the budget-scoring duty from OMB to the Democrat-controlled CBO, was an outright repudiation of a key part of that act. If this trend continues, all of the discipline potentially achieved in the famous "agreement" of October 1990 will slip away. A specific danger area is the manipulation of "economic and technical corrections" to allow more spending whenever the act's categorical ceilings threaten to put Congress on a spending diet.

## REFORM SIX: ADOPT THE BUDGET PROCESS REFORM ACT

The budget enforcement provisions of 1990, coupled with the reform of budget accounting itself, would be significant improvements. But, thanks to the efforts of Rep. Chris Cox (R-CA), there is an even more sweeping reform on the table. Cox's reform act is brilliantly devised to encourage those who tend naturally to do the wrong thing—members of Congress—to do the right thing.

Cox's plan would begin by establishing in law by May 5 of each year a budget resolution containing only 19 numbers, one for each of the major policy or appropriation areas. This would be a joint resolution signed into law by the president. The only exemptions would be Social Security and interest on the national debt. After adoption of the budget law, the president would present his detailed proposals, and Congress would adopt individual appropriations bills within the budget law ceilings.

If Congress passed an appropriation bill exceeding the ceiling, however, a two-thirds vote of each house of Congress would be required. The president would be given enhanced rescission authority with respect to any amounts over the budget law ceiling; Congress would have a chance to override each reduced item. Agency heads would be required to make up plans for how entitlement funds would be allocated in case the resulting appropriation fell short of requirements.

If Congress could not get its act together and pass a budget law before May 15, the president automatically would get rescission authority over any subsequently passed amount over the previous year's budget. And the passage of the budget law would require a two-thirds vote in each house. This would give Congress a powerful incentive to stay on schedule.

What if Congress couldn't pass its appropriations bills by the October 1 budget deadline? Then an automatic continuing resolution would go into effect, authorizing only the same amount as was spent in the previous year. (This would be worthwhile even if the rest of the Cox plan were not adopted.) The CBO would be the scorekeeper.

The Cox plan as revised in late 1991 now incorporates the enhanced rescission proposal (Reform Four) and does away with the current services budget (Gimmick 3).

Former Office of Personnel Management Director Donald Devine has written that "all the Cox proposal does is make Congress live up to deadlines it has already set for the budget process. It's a brilliant idea, and responsible congressmen should be pleased at the external discipline this would place on their voting decisions. As for the others, the taxpayers should know who they are so they could apply some heat. Mr. Cox surely has given them the blowtorch."

## REFORM SEVEN: ADOPT A SPENDING CONTROL AMENDMENT

Ordinarily this proposal is called the "balanced budget" amendment, and its underlying principles and various provisions are well described in Lewis K. Uhler's book, *Setting Limits: Constitutional Control of Government.* The idea here is to establish in the Constitution some brake on perpetual deficit spending and, depending on the version, a limit on taxation. Perhaps the Cox Budget Process Reform Act would suffice; it is certainly worth a serious try. But the idea of a constitutional limitation on spending and taxing ought to be kept on the table, if for no other reason than to keep the pressure on Congress to do something responsible before the hammer comes down. (The 1990 version of the amendment was defeated in the House. The vote was 279 in favor to 150 opposed, just seven votes short of the required two-thirds vote.)

The generic "balanced budget" amendment relies on the adoption each year by Congress of a statement of projected revenues and expenses, which would have to be in balance. In some versions, a deficit can be projected only with a supermajority vote in House or Senate. In others, there is a tax-limitation provision that prevents Congress from meeting balanced budget goals by the simple expedient of raising taxes.

An alternative proposal deserving serious consideration focuses not on a "statement" adopted by Congress—whose "statements" are not to be believed by intelligent people—but on the act of issuing more gross federal debt. In this version, a dollar limit, like $5 trillion, is set in the Constitution, and when that limit is reached no government official can authorize the issuance of any additional bonds, notes or bills. A different version (Armstrong-Boren) would allow the issuance of additional debt only with a supermajority vote in Congress. (If $5 trillion seems too large and far away, consider that in 1990 Congress set a new statutory debt ceiling of $4.145 trillion, which will be reached before the end of 1993.)

The debt limit approach has the great virtues of avoiding "statements" of Congress and achieving self-enforcement. Were the specified limit reached, no more debt could be issued. If the Treasury Secretary signed indentures on additional bonds, conservative Wall Street bond counsels would simply decline to certify them as validly issued debt instruments, and typical bond buyers would decline to buy them. The Treasury might survive for a while selling small-denomination savings bonds to individuals, or special securities to foreign buyers, but that could not go on for long. The unmarketability of securities issued after reaching of the debt limit would force some action: either a balanced budget or a sale of excess government assets (only a temporary solution). If the debt limit amendment included a tax limitation clause, the only viable long-run alternative would be to restrain federal spending. This would be a fiscal responsibility provision with "great white shark" teeth.

Such a program of accounting and budget reform, added to the new financial management tools described in Chapter 3, would at last bring some badly needed good sense and fiscal responsibility into a badly flawed process.

# Chapter Eight

# CUTTING THE CARD

"WHENEVER THE PEOPLE are well informed . . . and things get so far wrong as to attract their notice, they may be relied upon to set them right." So spoke Thomas Jefferson, the apostle of American democracy, at the time of the ratification of the American Constitution. A strong proponent of civic activism, he spoke approvingly of Shay's Rebellion, in which armed Massachusetts agrarians marched to the Springfield Court House for redress of grievances. And he made a continuing apology for the excesses of the French Revolution.

But when Mr. Jefferson became president, he had cause to reassess his earlier enthusiasm for citizen protest. In 1807 he secured passage of the Embargo Act, prohibiting trade with Great Britain and its colony, Canada. The people of Northern New England openly disobeyed and ridiculed the act, and mocked the few customs officials who dared to try to enforce it along the Canadian border. When dozens of Vermont town meetings demanded its repeal, President Jefferson ruefully observed that he had "felt the foundations of government shaken" in a manner that could "overrule the Union."

The same citizen defiance of government has broken out many times in our history: against the 1828 "Tariff of Abominations"; against the Fugitive Slave Act and the extension of slavery into

"Bleeding Kansas"; against the shameful segregation of Black Americans; and against withholding income tax on interest accrued to bank savings accounts. Most recently, the people have risen up to defeat (albeit briefly) the congressional pay grab of 1989.

The "pay grab" incident illustrates how citizen power in our age can defeat outrages perpetrated in Washington. On December 13, 1989 the Quadrennial Commission on Executive, Legislative and Judicial Salaries issued its report on pay increases for, among others, members of Congress. The Commission recommended congressional pay increases from $89,500 to $135,000 a year. Under a provision concocted in 1985 to protect congressmen from the heat of increasing their own pay, the Quad Commission recommendations, once approved by the president, would automatically go into effect without a vote, unless Congress acted to disapprove this expansion of its own benefits within 30 days.

In 1987, for instance, the Quad Commission and the president recommended a 16% pay increase. The Senate voted to disapprove it, but the leadership of the House contrived to delay the House vote until the 31st day. The House, of course, then voted strongly against its own pay increase—one day after the deadline, so it had no effect. Both House and Senate went home with fatter paychecks, and most of its members could crow to their constituents about voting against the pay raise even as they were licking their lips over their fattened paychecks.

When the 1989 pay hike came around, outgoing President Reagan passed up his chance to reduce the increases to a reasonable level, and headed home to California. President Bush, in turn, ducked the issue. Unless Congress acted to defeat the pay raise by February 7, the deal was done. The Senate had passed a resolution of disapproval, but the leadership of the House, notably Speaker Jim Wright, announced that there would be no opportunity for a House vote to disapprove the pay raise until after the deadline.

Meanwhile, a firestorm had started to build among the people who would have to pay the bills for the pay raise—not only the immediate salary costs, but also the inflated retirement benefit package tied to the salaries (Speaker Wright, for example, would realize a million dollars in increased pension benefits from the 50% pay raise). Editorials thundered against it. The phone lines on radio talk shows crackled with cries of outrage. Letters to editors vilified every person involved in this shabby scheme, Republican and Democrat. Bags of mail and thousands of phone calls converged on Congress. National publications such as *Human Events* trumpeted the pay grab on their front pages. The National Taxpayers Union fanned the flames through direct mail and media events. Tens of thousands of Americans sent their representatives tea bags, reminders of the Boston Tea Party, with a concise message attached: "Read My Lips: NO Pay Raise." The heat was on—really on!

But Jim Wright and his allies (of both parties) held fast. All they had to do was stall until midnight on February 7, and the money was in the bank. Since Wright controlled the Rules Committee, the Senate-passed resolution of disapproval could be safely bottled up.

Wright, however, underestimated the resourcefulness of one of Congress' great taxpayer champions, Rep. Bill Dannemeyer (R-CA). On February 6 he threw the House into a panic by introducing a new resolution requiring the House to vote before the deadline on the resolution of disapproval. The trick was to force a vote on it. Dannemeyer moved that his resolution be treated as a "privileged matter," entitled to precedence. Rep. Thomas Foley (now Speaker) was in the chair at the moment. He contrived to delay a ruling. But under House rules a privileged motion must be given priority over other House activity. Dannemeyer had previously reserved one minute to address the House, and now he used it to inform the House that, one way or another, there would be a vote on the pay raise that day or the next.

Dannemeyer had the pay-raisers where he wanted them. If his motion were ruled privileged, he would have an up-or-down vote on the pay raise. If the Chair denied his request for privilege, there would be a roll call vote appealing the denial. And if the leadership moved to adjourn, he would insist on a roll call on that motion.

The Democratic leadership then moved to adjourn. But the members, having been told very clearly by Dannemeyer that the upcoming vote was, in effect, the pay-raise vote, defeated the adjournment motion 238–88. The following day, Dannemeyer's pay grab disapproval resolution passed 380–48. It was rushed to the Senate, where it was approved 94–6. The pay raise crashed in flames. The people had won a rare victory over the business-as-usual politicians.

The victory was short-lived, however. Nine months later the pay grabbers succeeded in getting a 40% pay hike by using some of the most underhanded tactics ever seen in a place famous for them—"a House of ill repute."

Within three days of the new pay grab's unveiling in November 1989, the bill was whisked through both houses of Congress and signed into law. Congressional leaders had learned the hard way that a naked pay raise—not masked by other provisions—would fail. So this time the grab was cloaked in something labelled "the Government Ethics Reform Act of 1989." Congressmen could return home and tell their constituents that they had staunchly backed reform of "government ethics" (which sounds to most people like a patent contradiction in terms, like "jumbo shrimp").

To further cover up this charade, the Republican and Democratic congressional campaign committees and the two parties' national committees made a quiet "non-aggression pact." A copy of the pact found its way into the hands of Citizens for a Sound Economy, which published excerpts in its June 1990 bulletin. The key clause: "The vote on (this bill) is not an appropriate point of criticism in the coming campaigns. We will publicly oppose the use of this issue in any campaign in the 1990 cycle." The two campaign committees even agreed to withhold campaign funds from challengers in 1990 congressional races who would make this lightning pay grab an issue against incumbents. National columnist Robert Novak, speaking later at Hillsdale College, had this to say about this reprehensible scam: "The Republican and Democratic congressional leadership made a deal which, if the Sherman Antitrust Act had been heeded, would have sent them all to prison. . . . I have been covering Washington politics for almost forty years, but it was not until then that I knew that the whole system was and is irredeemably corrupt. . . ."

Two members of Congress who apparently agreed are Hank Brown (R-CO) and Andrew Jacobs (D-IN). On August 2, 1990 they introduced a bill to repeal the 1989 pay raise and put congressional salaries back to $89,500, while preserving the other "ethics" reforms contained in the 1989 act. At a news conference announcing the legislation, Brown was joined by Citizens for a Sound Economy, Citizens Against Government Waste, the National Taxpayers Union, Coalitions for America, and Ralph Nader's Congressional Accountability Project.

"No company in this nation would hand out a 25 percent pay raise to their employees if they were more than $3 trillion in debt,"

Brown said. "Yet on the heels of raising our debt limit, and when the federal government continues to dig the nation into a deeper financial crisis, its top elected and appointed officials ask for more money. Fiscal responsibility has fallen to the wayside." Added Alan Keyes, president of Citizens Against Government Waste, "There is only one way for ordinary citizens to deal with this irresponsible behavior. If Congress does not reverse this hypocrisy . . . the American people . . . will have the final word in November."

UNFORTUNATELY, THE AMERICAN people did not take it out on the salary grabbers in November 1990. And so, emboldened, the Senate came back in 1991 with yet another grab. On July 17, a day that, like Pearl Harbor Day, should live in infamy, the Senate by a 53–45 margin voted its members a $23,100 pay raise "to achieve parity with the House." It did so unannounced, beginning at 8:47 P.M., after most of the national press corps had headed home for the day. By 9:50 P.M. the deed was done. The "Stealth pay raise," as *Washington Times* columnist Clarence Page called it, took effect not after the 1992 election, but as soon as it was approved by the House and signed by the president.

The National Taxpayers Union calculated, in addition, that the pay raise could boost a senator's lifetime congressional pension by anywhere from $325,000 to $2 million. Unlike most private sector retirement plans, the congressional retirement benefits are fully indexed for inflation. If he retires in January 1995, at the end of his present term, Sen. Robert Byrd (D-WV), the architect of the pay raise, will receive an annual pension of $111,800, almost $20,000 more than he would have been entitled to without the raise and more than the pre-raise level for active Senate service.

In November 1992 the people will get a chance to pass judgment on some of those senators who voted themselves this lavish pay increase. But punishing these miscreants in November 1992 is not enough.

## CITIZENS MUST DRIVE REFORMS

America sorely needs a people-power coalition to bring our national government back under control—not just on one burning issue like the pay raise, but on the whole question of the shabby, dishonest, disgraceful way our government runs its business.

I am not calling—here—for a coalition to cut government waste or to reduce the size of the federal government. Nor am I calling—here—for tax reductions. I do support the efforts of many groups like the Citizens for a Sound Economy, National Taxpayers Union, and Citizens Against Government Waste, who embrace those particular goals. But the overarching, crying need is to generate an explosion of citizen demand for a government which is not only up front and candid, but *honest with its numbers*.

**So long as the federal government—Congress and the executive branch—go on falsifying the true accounting of our nation's taxing and spending, none of us can have any clear idea of where we stand and what we must do. Honest accounting, the essence of public accountability, is at the heart of every needed reform.**

One of the glories of America's history is the degree to which—with the one awful exception that culminated in the Civil War—Americans see their national government as legitimate and honorable. We may argue about whether to spend more on defense or on Social Security or on food stamps. We may go at each other hammer and tongs over who should bear the burden of higher taxes, if any. But at a level beyond those issues there has been a consensus that our national government "adds up" all right. The unhappy truth is that our government doesn't add up any more, and a growing number of people are coming to realize it.

How can a citizen have any respect for his or her national government when it is clear that its financial accounts have been doctored, fudged and distorted solely to serve the interests of those in power? Or pledge allegiance to a government that silently and covertly adds hundreds of billions of dollars of future liabilities—which are never reflected in its financial accounts and statements? Or part peacefully with tax dollars when the government permits billions of dollars to wander about its financial landscape without effective information and controls over where it goes?

Imagine yourself at an annual meeting of a large corporation in which you are a stockholder. Suppose the corporation's accountants report to you that the corporation can't pass an audit, has disguised or failed to record billions of dollars worth of accrued liabilities in its books, regularly uses phony economic figures, and has no chief financial officer. After the initial shock wore off, you probably would vote to dump the management at once. If that failed, you would be on the phone to your broker to unload your stock as fast as you could.

That's just where we are with the federal government. There are over a hundred million taxpayers who are, in a sense, shareholders in this multi-trillion-dollar enterprise. When they find out how their government is cheating on the basic information they need to make intelligent decisions, they will probably vent their fury just as they did on the 1989 pay raise issue. They certainly should!

At risk here is continued support of our national government by the great middle class, the people who hold the jobs, run the businesses, own the homes and pay the taxes. Once confronted with the facts, they'll see that their prosperity and security are intertwined with what our leaders in Washington do with the power "we the people" have conferred upon them. They cannot help but understand that the mistakes we make today will become the ugly surprises for our innocent children and grandchildren, who will be called upon to pay the bills.

As a CPA, this is crystal clear to me. But you don't have to be trained in accounting to understand that Thomas Jefferson was right when he said to James Madison that "the accounts of the United States ought to be, and may be made, as simple as those of a common farmer, and capable of being understood by common farmers." As president, he instructed his Treasury Secretary Albert Gallatin:

> If . . . there can be added a simplification of the form of accounts in the Treasury Department, and in the organization of its officers, so as to bring everything to a single centre, we might hope to see the finances of the Union as clear and intelligible as a merchant's books, so that every member of Congress, and every man of any mind in the Union, should be able to comprehend them, to investigate abuses, and consequently to control them.

**Mr. Jefferson had the right idea. Unless the people can control their government, it is no longer theirs. And until the government is made to account honestly, fairly and openly for what it does with the money it spends today and holds for the future, the government is not under the control of the people. It is time, indeed past time, for those who stand for truth in government to create a "Truth in Government" coalition to bring about some fundamental reform. That coalition will include groups fighting government**

waste and abuse, groups representing the taxpayers, groups of businesses small and large, good government groups, and just about everyone who is not a party to or a beneficiary of the present web of fiscal deception.

The Bush Administration is promising more vigorous initiatives toward honest accounting and good financial management. Its 1991 budget asked for funds for more audits and investigations of government spending. It also asked for $3 million (.00024 %, almost an invisible amount in a budget of $1.223 trillion in outlays) to improve the workings of the Federal Managers Financial Integrity Act. Those funds will support a tough program to link internal control review and reporting to the budget. They also will promote senior agency management involvement in the internal control process, and follow up on efforts to correct shortcomings. That's a start in the right direction. The 1992 budget document reports encouraging progress, candidly lists 117 "high-risk areas" and details the steps being taken to get the problems under control.

A Truth in Government coalition would present a list of specific steps and get every member of Congress to "take the pledge" to support them. Many of the items in this list have been described in earlier chapters:

1. Accrual or "liability" accounting in place of cash accounting
2. Capital budgeting
3. Redefinition of the budget into general, trust fund, and enterprise accounts
4. Honest, realistic economic projections, openly arrived at
5. Biennial budget cycles
6. Strong enforcement of the 1990 Budget Enforcement Act provisions
7. Congressional budget process reform
8. A strongly supported and independent Chief Financial Officer
9. Auditing of the federal government's activities by independent, "outside" Certified Public Accountants
10. An honest and understandable annual financial statement to citizens and taxpayers

Note that I have left off two proposals that I urged in Chapter 7: enhanced rescission authority or line-item veto, and a balanced budget-type constitutional amendment. I have done so because they are political devices to curb the growth of the federal government and expand the power of the president vis-à-vis Congress over spending decisions. As such, they are not in the same category as the ten honest budgeting, accounting and financial management issues listed above. They comprise a core of non-ideological proposals relating to process, reporting, accounting and financial management. Even those who urge more federal spending and taxing can in good conscience sign on to this reform package—unless they hope to advance their own interests at the expense of honesty, openness and good government. The present workings of the federal government afford ample opportunity for stealthy maneuvers. Those who delight in promoting their special interests through sneaky and dishonest gimmickry will oppose a citizens' movement for honest accounting and fiscal responsibility. As politicians are sometimes said to pray, "Let my opponents be dishonest, venal, arrogant and underhanded, Lord, that I may look the better."

## DEMANDING TRUTH IN GOVERNMENT

It is time that concerned citizens put together a truly irresistible movement to tell our elected officials loud and clear that we're onto their financial deceit, and won't stand for it one day longer. How would such a national "Truth in Government" citizens' movement work? Here are a few suggestions for action:

• *Action One:* Develop and publish a very specific "honest budgeting credo" for members of Congress, containing the essential proposals and practices. This would go beyond useless generalities like "support honest budgeting" to spell out specific requirements such as "vote to sustain points of order against budget resolutions containing unspecified savings or obviously unrealizable program changes."

• *Action Two:* Individually invite every member of Congress to publicly subscribe to this credo. A "Dear Colleague" letter from respected and influential senior members of both parties urging other members to get on board would be very helpful.

• *Action Three:* Mobilize its influential membership in the home districts of signers to offer political support and approbation to the signers for taking this important commitment—and put the heat on those who won't take the pledge, through personal communications, letters to the editor, etc. The goal, however, would not be punishment so much as inspiration to get on board. Members of this action group might include accounting, political science and law students at colleges around the country.

• *Action Four:* Organize a Truth in Government Caucus in Congress, which would meet occasionally to review current budgetary gimmicks and plan a legislative strategy for defeating them. It would also educate members on honest accounting, budgeting and financial management proposals emanating from the Comptroller General, the Inspectors General, the Controller and the agency CFOs, and professional groups like the Government Accounting Standards Board, the Association of Government Accountants, and the American Institute of CPAs.

• *Action Five:* When some unconscionably dishonest budget or accounting gimmick makes its appearance, mobilize citizens to oppose it by pressuring Congress directly and through the news media. Similarly, organize expert testimony and public support for needed improvements in budgeting and financial management, especially including the Comptroller General's reports, which are little noticed outside of Washington (and all too often ignored inside).

• *Action Six:* Create an ongoing and knowledgeable "Shadow Budget Committee" to prepare annual reports on progress in budgeting honesty, just like Freedom House's annual reports on the progress of freedom around the world. There is already a "Shadow Open Market Committee," which critiques the Federal Reserve System's open market operations, and a "Shadow Financial Regulatory Committee," which keeps track of the financial regulators as they confront the S&L and commercial bank crises.

• *Action Seven:* Lavish honors on those members of Congress, Inspectors General, GAO officials and others who have done good works for this cause. A well-publicized award to a member of Congress as a "Champion of Honest Budgeting" will be much appreciated when he or she seeks reelection—especially when local citizens write letters to the editor reminding the public that "Congressman Jones won a coveted award for insisting that we be told the truth about how Congress spends our money." (Take it from me: Congressmen are extremely grateful for such spontaneous commendation in the news media!) On the flip side, announcing "Budget Cheater of the Year" awards to Congress' worst performers ought to cause a lot of discomfort among the malefactors.

Citizens can improve government if their concerns are carefully and shrewdly acted upon. The ideas mentioned above are aimed at Congress, but a similar program could be developed for citizen budget watchers in states, counties and cities across the country, Indeed, there are some taxpayers' associations and state public policy institutes which have moved or are moving in this direction.

When I speak on this subject I often use a small but potent story to emphasize the need for acting now: "A frog was put into a tank of water at room temperature. Then the water temperature was raised ever so slightly each day. Each day the frog noticed little difference from the day before, but eventually, the frog boiled to death. It didn't know enough to jump out! That's about what Congress is doing to the American people by its mishandling of the budget and financial management systems of government. It is steadily boiling us in a stew of cooked numbers." **The penalty for complacency, like that of the frog, grows larger and more dangerous every day—as does the bill our children will have to pay if we fail to act. Isn't it about time we hopped out of the tank—and got control of the heat—before it's too late?**

Earlier in this book I described "The Most Expensive Credit Card in the World." If members of Congress are going to have the use of such a card, the people must demand that it be used honestly. For those members of Congress determined to keep using their card irresponsibly, fudging the numbers, and covering up the hard truth from the people, there is only one solution: the people must take back their cards—permanently.

The time has come. We, the people, owe it to ourselves and to the America we love, to act—and to act *now.*

97

# APPENDIX

JOSEPH J. DioGUARDI
20ᵀᴴ DISTRICT NEW YORK

COMMITTEES
BANKING, FINANCE AND
URBAN AFFAIRS

GOVERNMENT OPERATIONS

SELECT COMMITTEE ON NARCOTICS
ABUSE AND CONTROL

**Congress of the United States**
**House of Representatives**
**Washington, DC** 20515

WASHINGTON OFFICE
325 CANNON BUILDING
WASHINGTON DC 20515
(202) 225-6506

DISTRICT OFFICE
1 NORTH BROADWAY, SUITE 901
WHITE PLAINS, NY 10601
(914) 997-6440

May 28, 1987

The Honorable Howard H. Baker
Chief of Staff
The White House
1600 Pennsylvania Avenue, N.W.
Washington, D.C. 20500

Dear Senator Baker:

Your interest in budget reform is very encouraging. And I believe this is a viable issue for President Reagan to take the offensive against those who claim the Reagan legacy is one of deficits when, in fact, it is not.

Did you know that when using Generally Accepted Accounting Principles (GAAP) the budget deficit during Jimmy Carter's last year in office was higher than the deficit in 1984, the last year of President Reagan's first term? Using 1984 dollars, the deficit in 1980 was $408 billion; in 1984, the deficit was $333 billion -- a cut in the deficit of $75 billion.

In addition, when using GAAP, President Reagan is lowering deficits as a percentage of GNP from the Carter levels. In 1980, the deficit was 12.5% of GNP; in 1984, the deficit was 9.3% of GNP.

Budget reform must be viewed in the larger context of financial management. As important as the budget process is, we will never be able to solve our financial problems without a comprehensive solution. There is also the need for:

- Sound accounting principles to properly measure costs.

- Sound information systems to establish control over operations.

- Sound reporting to measure results and reward accomplishments.

- Sound organization to assure proper implementation of these keys to successful financial management.

This is a logical issue for President Reagan and there is still time to put this fundamental reform into place.

A portion of the cash-basis deficits we are experiencing represent the liquidation of liabilities incurred many years ago, when the programs were first enacted. If those liabilities had been recorded in the period incurred, deficits would be lower under President Reagan than under Jimmy Carter.

100

The Honorable Howard H. Baker
Page 2
May 28, 1987


The following graphs using constant dollars and
the accrual basis of accounting, which is a more meaningful
measure of spending, clearly show that deficits compiled by Jimmy
Carter are greater than the deficits incurred under President
Reagan.

The Carter Years:

| | Cash Basis Annual Deficit | | | GAAP Basis Annual Deficit | | |
|---|---|---|---|---|---|---|
| | | ($ Billions) | | | | |
| Year | Nominal $ | % GNP | 1984 $ | Nominal $ | % GNP | 1984 $ |
| 1977 | $ 53.6 | 2.9% | $ 85.9 | $224.6 | 12.1% | $359.8 |
| 1978 | 59.0 | 2.8 | 88.4 | 215.8 | 10.3 | 323.2 |
| 1979 | 40.2 | 1.7 | 55.5 | 256.8 | 10.9 | 354.9 |
| 1980 | 73.8 | 2.9 | 93.5 | 322.2 | 12.5 | 408.3 |
| | | | | | 11.45% | $1446.2 |
| | | | | | Avg. | |

The Reagan Years:

| | Cash Basis Annual Deficit | | | GAAP Basis Annual Deficit | | |
|---|---|---|---|---|---|---|
| | | ($ Billions) | | | | |
| Year | Nominal $ | % GNP | 1984 $ | Nominal $ | % GNP | 1984 $ |
| 1981 | $ 78.9 | 2.7% | $ 91.3 | $ 264.7 | 9.2% | 306.3 |
| 1982 | 127.9 | 4.2 | 138.5 | 314.0 | 10.3 | 339.9 |
| 1983 | 207.8 | 6.4 | 215.6 | 395.3 | 12.3 | 410.1 |
| 1984 | 185.3 | 5.2 | 185.3 | 333.4 | 9.3 | 333.4 |
| | | | | | 10.28% | $1389.7 |
| | | | | | Avg. | |

Source: Arthur Andersen & Co.


As you can see, Jimmy Carter's deficits are more than $55
billion greater than the debt incurred during President Reagan's
first term.
Without that initiative we in the minority will not be able to
push this issue to the fore in time for President Reagan to
preside over its implementation.

My professional background as a Certified Public Accountant
led me to introduce H.R. 1241, legislation to create a Chief
Financial Officer of the United States. I would be more than
happy to provide you with any additional material that you may
need.

Sincerely,

Joseph J. DioGuardi
Member of Congress

JOSEPH J DIOGUARDI
' 20TH DISTRICT NEW YORK

COMMITTEES
MERCHANT MARINE AND FISHERIES

GOVERNMENT OPERATIONS

SELECT COMMITTEE ON NARCOTICS
ABUSE AND CONTROL

# Congress of the United States
## House of Representatives
### Washington, DC 20515

WASHINGTON OF
375 CANNON BU
WASHINGTON DC
(202) 225-61

DISTRICT OFFI
1 NORTH BROADWAY,
WHITE PLAINS NY
(914) 997-84

June 24, 1987

The Honorable Richard B. Cheney
U.S. Representative
Cannon House Office Building
Room 104
Washington, D.C. 20515

Dear Dick:

As requested, I will attempt to summarize the principal
reasons why the Federal deficit as determined on the accrual-
basis of accounting (as presented in my letter to Howard Baker
dated May 28, 1987, copy enclosed) differs with the cash-basis
deficit calculation the Federal government now employs. The
former is based on generally accepted accounting principles
(GAAP) that government already imposes on public companies in the
private sector through the S.E.C.; the latter is the "Mickey
Mouse" cash accounting system we took New York City off in the
mid-seventies as a condition for the Federal bailout, but that
the U.S. Government still uses itself!!

Morton Egol, who heads up the public sector industry
practice at Arthur Andersen & Co. (AA & Co.), the international
accounting firm, said in a March 10, 1987 Wall Street Journal
article:

"Cash-basis accounting, which the Federal government uses,
is an oxymoron. It is merely a reporting of checkbook
entries with virtually no assessment of assets and
liabilities and no evaluation of outputs. Unlike accrual-
basis accounting, cash-basis accounting ignores such things
as accounts receivable and accounts payable. It provides no
reserves for uncollectible debts, treats the sale of assets
as income and long-term capital investments as current
expenses, fails to depreciate capital assets, and disregards
the long-term cost of retirement programs."

Since the government does not maintain accrual-basis
accounting systems, there can be no precise determination of the
accrual-basis Federal deficit. AA & Co. performed a study of
U.S. Government accounting practices in 1975 and produced the
first set of accrual-basis financial statements for the Federal
government as of the fiscal 1974 year-end (see copy of FY 84
statement enclosed). Subsequently, a Commission was formed by
U.S. Treasury Secretary Bill Simon that reviewed the results of
this study and developed a methodology to carry-forward the
results of the AA & Co. study so that, for each year since, the

102

The Honorable Richard B. Cheney
Page 2
June 24, 1987

U.S. Treasury has prepared prototype accrual-basis financial statements.

As confirmed by a recent update of the 1974 study and AA & Co. publication released in February 1986, "Sound Financial Reporting In the U.S. Government," such financial statements represent the best indication available of the real cost of government and the accumulated deficit after reflecting all known liabilities. (A copy of the AA & Co. booklet is enclosed for your reference.)

The AA & Co. updated study confirmed an accrual-basis deficit for fiscal 1984 of $333 billion as compared with $185 billion on a cash-basis, a variance of $148 billion. The financial statements in the publication include a statement on page 17 which summarizes the differences between accrual-basis and cash-basis accounting for the Federal budget. As shown in that statement, the principal causes of the higher annual-basis deficits are:

|  |  | $ Billions |
|---|---|---|
| - | Depreciation | 30 |
| - | Provision for Social Security | 133 |
| - | Provision for Pensions | 61 |
| - | Additions to Property & Equipment | (72) |
| - | Miscellaneous, Net | ( 4) |
|  | Excess of Accrual-Basis Deficit Over the Cash-Basis Deficit | 148 |

The following is a brief description of the above items, which are discussed in more detail in the booklet:

Depreciation--The wear and tear on long-lived assets is charged to the period in which the assets are in service.

Social Security Provision--The unfunded liability for government promises to participants in the social security program, net of expected contributions from participants, is reflected in the accrual-basis financial statements and is being amortized over 30 years. This is the method of accounting followed for retirement programs in the private sector. The accrued liability at September 30, 1984 was $1.9 trillion and represents the amounts promised to present participants that will have to be funded by contributions from future participants. It is a form of borrowing.

The Honorable Richard B. Cheney
Page 3
June 24, 1987

**Pensions Provision**--As for social security, the government makes no provision for amounts it has promised military or civilian personnel under various pension programs. The above amount represents the true cost of personnel services in excess of the current salary portion of personnel costs. The accrued liability for such programs was $1.3 trillion at September 30, 1984.

**Property**--The cash-basis of accounting does not distinguish between operating expenses and long-lived assets. Under GAAP, such assets are capitalized and then depreciated over their estimated useful lives, thereby apportioning the cost over the periods benefitted by the expenditure.

There are many accounting issues that should be resolved to refine the accrual-basis/GAAP financial statements. For example, the government's receivables should be reduced to reflect provisions for bad debt losses on loans to farmers, students, etc., liabilities under various credit guaranty and insurance programs should be recorded, and accounting policies for programs that have grown in significance since 1974, such as medicare, should be re-evaluated. The resolution of such issues would tend to widen the difference in the accrual-basis and cash-basis deficit.

In my letter to Howard Baker I explained that while accrual basis/GAAP deficits are considerably larger than the cash deficits for the reasons outlined above, Jimmy Carter's aggregate accrual basis deficits are even $55 billion greater than those incurred in Ronald Reagan's first term. The main reason for this is that President Reagan spent proportionately more on capital items whose benefit gets amortized over future fiscal periods under GAAP. Conversely, President Carter spent proportionately more on items which were consumed immediately, providing no benefit to future periods. Furthermore, President Carter's budgets incurred future obligations to spend which were not recorded as Carter deficits under the cash basis. As a result, much of President Reagan's cash basis deficit is actually the accrual basis deficit of Jimmy Carter.

I believe that failure by the government to follow sound financial reporting is not merely an accounting issue, it's governmental as well. It is a crucial question of governance -- a missing link in our constitutional system that allows public officials to commit resources without reporting to the public. This lack of public accountability has resulted in fiscal recklessness and an unstable economic environment that threatens

The Honorable Richard B. Cheney
Page 4
June 24, 1987


the foundations of our society. The lack of public
accountability fosters cynicism among the citizenry and can
weaken the nation's resolve and its ability to act appropriately
when challenges arise.

The notion that the Federal government should improve its
accounting practices is not new. As Thomas Jefferson said in a
letter to the Secretary of the Treasury in 1802:

> "I think it an object of great importance. . .to simplify
> our system of finance, and to bring it within the
> comprehension of every member of Congress. . .the whole
> system (has been) involved in impenetrable fog. There is a
> point. . .on which I should wish to keep my eye. . .a
> simplification of the form of accounts. . . so as to bring
> everything to a single center; we might hope to see the
> finances of the Union as clear and intelligible as a
> merchant's books, so that every member of Congress, and
> every man of any mind in the Union, should be able to
> comprehend them to investigate abuses, and consequently to
> control them."

If citizens and creditors were to demand the financial
information to which they're clearly entitled, incentives
would be created for sound fiscal management and perhaps for
more enlightened political leadership. We would then see
better-informed decision-making that could set the brakes on
fiscal recklessness. Ultimately, effective reporting of
government activities should improve public confidence in
public officials. And maybe--just maybe--citizens might
feel less cynical about the idea that concerted action and
some personal sacrifice are still the requirements for
effective self-government.

Please let me know if you want to discuss this further.

Sincerely,

Joseph J. DioGuardi
Member of Congress


Enclosures (3)

JOSEPH J. DioGUARDI
20TH-DISTRICT NEW YORK

COMMITTEES
BANKING, FINANCE AND
URBAN AFFAIRS

GOVERNMENT OPERATIONS

SELECT COMMITTEE ON NARCOTICS
ABUSE AND CONTROL

## Congress of the United States
### House of Representatives
#### Washington, DC 20515

WASHINGTON OFFICE
325 CANNON BUILDING
WASHINGTON DC 20515
(202) 225-6506

DISTRICT OFFICE
1 NORTH BROADWAY SUITE
WHITE PLAINS NY 10601
(914) 997-6440

July 28, 1987

Mr. James Miller
Director
Office of Management and Budget
Executive Office Building
Washington, D.C. 20503

Dear Jim:

Many thanks for your thoughtful letter of June 23, 1987, responding to my suggestion that accrual accounting based on generally accepted accounting principles (GAAP) should be used for Federal budget and reporting purposes.

Although I am more enlightened by your reply, I am no less persuaded that accrual-basis accounting is essential if we are to establish public accountability. The Congress should not be allowed to enact programs without including the full cost of programs in the budget and in reports on the Government's financial condition.

You made several points (outlined below) to which I would like to reply.

"There are more drawbacks than benefits from across-the-board application of the accrual concepts to the budgets."

When it comes to the threshold issue of accountability, you can not compromise on the basic need for meaningful information. Cash-basis budgets are essential, but so is accrual-basis information. You can't run an organization without information on liquidity and cash flow requirements, but you also need information on costs and liabilities. U.S. Federal Securities laws require a full set of reports by publicly held corporations and it is right in doing so.

When ranking the "drawbacks" of accrual-basis accounting (of which I admit none), against its benefits as a prerequisite for fair and complete reporting and public accountability, you are raising relatively minor mechanical and educational problems against a basic requirement for an informed electorate necessary for effective self-government.

"Although shifting the entire budget to an accrual-basis has major drawbacks, there are benefits to selective use of the accrual concept. As a result accruals are used in three major areas."

106

Mr. James Miller
Page 2
July 28, 1987

This reminds me of the old phrase--you can't be half
pregnant. The result of this hybrid accounting is only greater
confusion in the public mind and more rather than less distrust
in government. We need one set of reports to show costs and
another set to show how the programs were financed. You can't
combine these different objectives into one report without
clouding the issue. When you record accruals for some pension
programs, but not other programs, what has been gained unless all
accruals are recorded?

A misleading report results because readers will either
believe that all costs are reflected or they will be unable to
gauge the actual level of costs. In any event, the "other"
section of the budget buries an offsetting amount in order to
reflect total cash outlays accurately.

Publishing accrual-basis data for selected programs as an
appendix to the budget just adds to the proliferation of data
without getting to the heart of the problem, which is to inform
the public on the total costs of programs. Just as a public
corporation must report earnings per share, the Federal
government should be required to report the total cost of
government programs.

The economic burden of government programs is spread widely
over individuals, corporations, users, etc., and future
generations. Only by reporting total costs can the public assess
the actions of those it has chosen to formulate public policy.
Including accrual data for programs like the TVA and the Post
Office as an Appendix to the President's budget, programs which
in the aggregate are insignificant to the total unrecorded
accruals, and claiming this is fair and meaningful reporting of
the total cost of government illustrates the problem--not the
solution.

The President's proposal to reform the Federal Credit
programs may never have been necessary if budgets had been
required to be on an accrual-basis in the years those programs
were adopted.

<u>"It appears that using FY1982-85 for President Reagan's First
Term might have a significant effect on your conclusions."</u>

While it can be argued that the incoming President should be
charged with responsibility for the first nine months of
operations, the key point is that an accumulated accrual-basis

*Appendix*

deficit of several trillion dollars was inherited by Ronald
Reagan and the annual accrual-basis deficits were on the average
larger under Carter than Reagan.

The main reason for this is that President Reagan spent
proportionately more on capital items whose benefit gets
amortized over future fiscal periods under GAAP. Conversely,
President Carter spent proportionately more on items which were
consumed immediately, providing no benefit to future periods.
Furthermore, President Carter's budgets incurred future
obligations to spend which were not recorded as Carter deficits
under the cash-basis. As a result, some of President Reagan's
cash-basis deficit is actually the accrual-basis deficit of Jimmy
Carter.

**"The additional workload and reporting burden...are major
obstacles."**

The overwhelming majority of professional business opinion
clearly demonstrates that the production of accurate
comprehensive financial data is a mandatory prerequisite towards
eliminating waste, achieving high levels of efficiency and
cutting costs. Furthermore, the Federal government requires
every publicly held corporation and State and local governments
to maintain accounting systems that report accrual-basis
information to the public in addition to the requirement for
cash-basis reporting systems. How then can you declare this to
be a major obstacle?

**"...estimates of deficits on an accrual-basis will vary
considerably depending on the assumptions used to estimate the
accrued deficit."**

The need for estimates is frequently cited as a reason for
not adopting accrual accounting. The fact that judgment is
required to be applied in assessing assets and liabilities is a
plus factor, not a minus. Under the present cash-basis system,
we have literally no information on costs. A recent Wall Street
Journal editorial referred to the suggestion by the chairman of
the Armed Services committee's proposal to stay within budget
guidelines by simply delaying the payment of bills for fourteen
days. Is it better to be criticized for apparent fiscal
gimmickry of the type New York City used before it defaulted,
than to make reasonable judgments which are audited currently?

It is because accrual-basis accounting deals with the
substance of events that estimates are necessary. If amounts are

*Appendix*

Mr. James Miller
Page 4
July 28, 1987


due to the government, they should be recorded as assets, but
only to the extent they are collectible. This requires an
analysis of the credit worthiness of the borrower, which
hopefully was performed at the time the loans were made. If
compensation includes pension obligations, that element should be
calculated and accrued, and charged to current operations. This
requires an estimate of the average working lives of employees
and other factors which management needs to properly manage the
affairs of government. The information needed to make accounting
estimates is nothing more than the basic facts needed to manage
government.

"<u>Accrual deficit outcomes are based upon standards that are not
fully developed or agreed upon and, therefore, are not supportive
of our need for consistent reporting.</u>"

This is merely an excuse. First, a commission established
in 1976 made up of leaders in the accounting profession (in and
out of government) did develop accounting standards for the
Federal government. Second, the General Accounting Office
(GAO) has promulgated accounting principles for the government.
These standards and principles can easily be re-evaluated and
continuously updated.

As I am sure you know, the Goverment Accounting Standards
Board (GASB) has been in operation for a few years and has
developed guidelines that can be of use to the Federal
government. At least one other major industrialized nation has
prepared consolidated financial statements on the accrual-basis
and we can learn from that effort. Also, the International
Federation of Accountants has started a project to promulgate
international accounting standards for government.

The fact that accounting conventions may change is a virtue
of accounting, not a liability. Whenever accounting conventions
change, the statements are re-cast to meet the Standard of
Consistency. If the statements are audited, the officials
responsible for their preparation need not worry over confusion
or lack of public confidence.

"<u>If the most recent Treasury/GAO assumptions and GAAP principles
are used, the accrued deficit for the same year is estimated at
$140 billion</u>" (as compared with the $333 billion in the Arthur
Andersen & Co. assumptions).

First, the GAO has not accepted Treasury's reclassification
of social security obligations to "contingent liability" status

109

Mr. James Miller
Page 5
July 28, 1987


(see paragraph 3 of page V of the 1985 prototype of Consolidated
Financial Statements).

Second, the facts that would cause a change in accounting of
this magnitude should be clearly understood by public
policymakers. Why is it that a document with a by-line on its
cover "...Treasury's commitment to full disclosure of financial
information to the the public" has over-ridden the unanimous
recommendation of a commission established in 1976 and the sole
description of social security obligations, the nation's largest
government program, is relegated to a line-item on page 30 of a
31 page document, without any information on how the amount was
calculated and the impact the change in accounting has on
comparative financial information? The amount of $2.059 trillion
appears to be computed on an inconsistent basis with the manner
in which the unfunded obligation was calculated in prior years.
(The unfunded liability at September 30, 1984, was $4.2
trillion).

There was no requirement to change the accounting for social
security so the inconsistent reporting you were concerned with
was not the result of lack of standards, but of a decision to
change the accounting treatment that had been followed for a
decade and endorsed unanimously by an independent body.

-------------------------------------------

There is little doubt in my mind that accrual-basis
budgeting and reporting is an idea whose time has come and that
publishing official and credible accrual-basis financial reports
should be the top priority of a Chief Financial Officer. The
Budget submission should include a cash-basis plan and an
accrual-basis plan using the same accounting principles followed
in the official annual report.

You can be sure that successive administrations will not
take the time to carefully allocate the accumulated deficit
Ronald Reagan inherited from prior administrations, going all the
way back to New Deal days. There is precious little time to
adopt accrual-basis accounting and set the record straight. If
this is not done, the opening balance in the "Accumulated
Deficit" section of the first Annual Report of the United States
Government to the American people will have Ronald Reagan's name
on it.

There is nothing as compatible with Ronald Reagan's
philosophy and the goals of his administration as the laying out

*Appendix*

of the financial facts and the use of what we have learned about
proper accounting in the private sector to tell the truth about
how big government really is in this nation.

Let's not paper over the problem!  Let's solve it!

Sincerely,

Joseph J. DioGuardi
Member of Congress

# SELECTED BILLS SPONSORED BY REP. JOSEPH J. DioGUARDI (1985–88)

### 1985

HRes 40    Require ²/₃ majority to increase statutory debt limit

HRes 60    Require House committees to review Grace Committee Report

HRes 347    Request president to submit recommendations to implement Grace Commission Report

HJR 18    Constitutional amendment: Line item veto

HJR 27    Constitutional amendment: Balanced budget

HJR 166    Constitutional amendment: Reform budget procedures

HR 748    Require biennial budgeting

HR 1247    Require Congress to put each spending item in a separate bill

HR 1257    Implement Grace Commission recommendations for Defense

HR 2164    Accelerate removal of Social Security Trust Funds from budget

HR 2262    Authorize Defense Department Inspector General to take extraordinary enforcement actions

| | |
|---|---|
| HR 2297 | Require each agency to implement Grace Commission recommendations and report to Congress |
| HR 3252 | Authorize presidential rescission of spending authority unless Congress overrides |
| HR 3520 | Require deficit control procedures (Gramm-Rudman Act) |
| HR 3886 | Require economic assumptions for Defense spending be the same as for the rest of the budget |
| HR 3887 | Require president to report on accuracy of prior year's inflation estimates |

## 1986

| | |
|---|---|
| HRes 525 | Implement recommendations of Blue Ribbon Commission on Defense Management |
| HCR 352 | Limit funds available to Congress for official mail costs |
| HR 4495 | Federal Financial Management Improvement Act |
| HR 4659 | Improve government debt collection practices |
| HR 5093 | Federal Account Practices Review Commission Act |
| HR 5113 | Implement Grace Commission recommendations for Defense Department |

## 1987

| | |
|---|---|
| HJR 8 | Constitutional amendment: Line item veto |
| HJR 9 | Constitutional amendment: Reform budget procedures |
| HJR 82 | Disapprove increase in congressional salaries |
| HJR 117 | Constitutional amendment: Line item veto |
| HR 33 | Provide for biennial federal budgeting, Gramm-Rudman amendments |
| HR 518 | Disapprove increase in congressional salaries |
| HR 1028 | HUD income verification act |
| HR 1241 | Chief Financial Officer Act |
| HR 1440 | Prevent members from using campaign funds for personal purposes |
| HR 1589 | Consolidation of Defense Department operations |
| HR 1606 | Requires federal government to use private sector contracting |
| HR 2287 | Federal Accounting Practices Review Committee |
| HR 2363 | Line item veto; separate enrollment of appropriations items |
| HR 3129 | Line item rescission authority |
| HR 3142 | Chief Financial Officer Act |

## 1988

| | |
|---|---|
| HRes 526 | House Public Review Board and Inspector General |
| HR 4149 | Budget information distributed with tax forms |
| HR 4396 | Exclude Social Security from Gramm-Rudman calculations |
| HR 4744 | Require operating and capital budgets, trust fund accounting reforms |
| HR 5187 | Prevent members from using campaign funds for personal purposes |
| HR 5240 | Prevent members from using campaign funds for personal purposes |

# ORGANIZATIONS OF INTEREST

*The following organizations are active, in various ways, in the field of government spending and taxing control.*

**American Enterprise Institute for Public Policy Research**
1150 17th St. NW, Washington DC 20036—202/862-5800
*National intellectual center for free-market and defense-oriented public policy research.*

**American Institute of Certified Public Accountants**
1455 Pennsylvania Ave. NW, Washington DC 20004—202/737-6600
*Professional organization for CPAs.*

**Association of Government Accountants**
601 Wythe St., Alexandria VA 22314—703/684-6931
*Professional association for accountants working in federal, state and local governments.*

**Brookings Institution**
1755 Massachusetts Ave. NW, Washington DC 20036—202/767-9000
*National public policy research center, with liberal-moderate orientation.*

117

**Cato Institute**
224 2nd St. SE, Washington DC 20003—202/546-0200
*Leading scholarly center for libertarian ideas.*

**Center for a Responsible Federal Budget**
220½ E St. NE, Washington DC 20002—202/547-4484
*Citizens group working for reduction in Federal budget deficits.*

**Citizens against Government Waste**
1301 Connecticut Ave. NW, Washington DC 20036—202/467-5300
*Citizens group promoting government implementation of Grace Commission reforms in federal management policies.*

**Citizens for a Sound Economy**
470 L'Enfant Plaza SW #7112, Washington DC 20024—202/488-8200
*Large organization of citizens working for spending restraint and tax limitation.*

**Citizens for Congressional Reform Foundation**
470 L'Enfant Plaza SW #7401, Washington DC 20024—202/488-8288
*Grassroots national organization focusing on waste, fraud and corruption in Congress.*

**Competitive Enterprise Institute**
233 Pennsylvania Ave. SE, Washington DC 20003—202/547-1010
*National organization working for limited government, free market and reduced government regulation.*

**Congressional Budget Office**
2d & D Sts. SW, Washington DC 20515—202/226-2621
*Serves as Congress' research staff for the budget process; prepares reports analyzing implications of budgetary choices. Controversial for alleged partisanship.*

**The Free Congress Foundation**
717 Second Street NE, Washington, DC 20002—202/546-3000
A non-profit, non-partisan, research and educational organization.

**Free the Eagle**
666 Pennsylvania Ave. SE #300, Washington DC 20003—202/543-6090
*Citizen's lobby working for reduced federal spending and sound money.*

**General Accounting Office**
Washington DC 20548—202/275-2812
*Headed by the Comptroller General, the GAO is Congress's accounting and audit agency. It publishes numerous reports on all aspects of federal government operations, including budgeting and financial management.*

**Heritage Foundation**
214 Massachusetts Ave. NE, Washington DC 20002—202/546-4400
*Leading free-market-oriented think tank; publishes regular "back-grounders" on federal spending practices and legislation.*

**House Budget Committee**
House Office Building, Washington DC 20515—202/226-7200

**National Tax Limitation Committee**
201 Massachusetts Ave. NE, Washington DC 20002—202/547-4196
*National organization working to enact balanced budget amendment to U.S. Constitution.*

**National Taxpayers Union**
713 Maryland Ave. NE, Washington DC 20002—202/543-1300
*National citizens' group working to reduce federal spending and taxation.*

**Senate Budget Committee**
Senate Office Building, Washington DC 20510—202/224-0642

**Truth In Government**
34 Locust Ave., Rye NY 10580—914/967-7410
*National organization established by former Congressman Joe DioGuardi in 1990 to educate decision-makers, news media and the American people about incompetent and duplicitous budgeting and accounting in government.*

# REFERENCES

Adams, James Ring. *Secrets of the Tax Revolt.* New York: Harcourt Brace Jovanovich, 1984.

_____ *The Big Fix: Inside the S&L Scandal.* New York: Wiley, 1989.

Bennett, James & DiLorenzo, Thomas. *Underground Government: The Off Budget Public Sector.* Washington: Cato Institute, 1984.

Boskin, Michael J. & Wildavsky, Aaron. *The Federal Budget: Economics and Politics.* San Francisco: Institute for Contemporary Studies, 1982.

Cogan, John F. and Muris, Timothy J., "The Great Budget Shell Game," *The American Enterprise,* Nov. 1990.

Collender, Stanley E. *The Guide to the Federal Budget: Fiscal 1992.* Washington: Urban Institute, 1991.

Hillsdale College, ed. *The Federal Budget: The Economic, Political and Moral Implications for a Free Society.* Champions of Freedom series, No. 13. Hillsdale, Mich.: Hillsdale College Press, 1990.

Jones, Gordon S. and Marini, John A., eds. *The Imperial Congress: Crisis in the Separation of Powers.* New York: Pharos Books, 1988.; see esp. Margaret N. Davis, "The Congressional Budget Mess," pp. 151–182.

Leonard, Herman B. *Checks Unbalanced: The Quiet Side of Public Spending.* New York: Basic Books, 1986.

Malkin, Lawrence. *The National Debt.* New York: Holt, 1987.

Mayer, Martin. *The Greatest Ever Bank Robbery.* New York: Scribners, 1990.

## References

Mills, Gregory B. and Palmer, John L., eds. *Federal Budget Policy in the 1980s*. Washington: Urban Institute, 1984.

Moore, Stephen. "Managing the Federal Budget" in Charles Heatherly and Burton Y. Pines, eds. *Mandate for Leadership III*. Washington: Heritage Foundation, 1989.

Moraglio, Joseph F. *The Federal Budget: Management's Perspective*. Westport, Conn.: Greenwood Press, 1986.

Ott, David J. and Attiat F. *Federal Budget Policy*. Washington: Brookings Institution, 1965.

Paine, James L. *The Culture of Spending*. San Francisco: Institute for Contemporary Studies, 1991.

Pearce, Trudy. *Cleaning Up Congress: A Citizen's Guide to Congressional Reform*. Washington: Citizens for Congressional Reform Foundation, 1991.

Penner, Rudolph G. and Abramson, Alan J., eds. *Broken Purse Strings: Congressional Budgeting 1974–88*. Washington: Urban Institute, 1988.

Schick, Allen. *Congress and Money: Budgeting, Spending and Taxing*. Washington: Urban Institute, 1980.

————. *The Capacity to Budget*. Washington: Urban Institute, 1990.

Simon, William E. *A Time for Truth*. New York: Berkley, 1978.

Stockman, David. *The Triumph of Politics: The Failure of the Reagan Revolution*. New York: Harper & Row, 1986.

Tierney, Cornelius E. *Handbook of Federal Accounting Practices*. Reading, Mass.: Addison-Wesley, 1982.

White, Joseph and Wildavsky, Aaron. *The Deficit and the Public Interest: The Search for Responsible Budgeting in the 1980s*. Berkeley: U. of California Press, 1989.

Wildavsky, Aaron. *The New Politics of the Budgetary Process*. Glenview: Scott Foresman, 1988.

# INDEX

## Index